THE DECLARATION
OF INDEPENDENCE

This essential new series features classic texts by key figures that took center stage during a period of insurrection. Each book is introduced by a major contemporary radical writer who shows how these incendiary works still have the power to inspire, to provoke and maybe to ignite new revolutions . . .

THE DECLARATION
OF INDEPENDENCE

THOMAS JEFFERSON

INTRODUCTION BY MICHAEL HARDT

ADDITIONAL MATERIAL
BY GARNET KINDERVATER

VERSO
London • New York

First published by Verso 2007
© Verso 2007
Introduction © Michael Hardt 2007
All rights reserved

1 3 5 7 9 10 8 6 4 2

Verso
UK: 6 Meard Street, London W1F 0EG
USA: 180 Varick Street, New York, NY 10014-4606
www.versobooks.com

Verso is the imprint of New Left Books

ISBN-13: 978-1-84467-157-1

British Library Cataloguing in Publication Data
A catalogue record for this book is available from the British Library

Library of Congress Cataloging-in-Publication Data
A catalog record for this book is available from the Library of Congress

Typeset in Bembo by Hewer Text UK Ltd, Edinburgh
Printed in USA by Courier Stoughton Inc.

CONTENTS

Republicanism and Self-Government

Native Americans and Black Slavery

INTRODUCTION

THOMAS JEFFERSON, OR, THE TRANSITION OF DEMOCRACY

Michael Hardt

It cannot but feel rather odd speaking about Thomas Jefferson, who occupies such a central position in the US national pantheon, in the same breath as Vladimir Lenin, Mao Zedong, and Fidel Castro as a figure of modern revolutionary thought. For almost a century, after all, the United States government has served as the principal anti-revolutionary force in the world, striving to suppress revolutionary movements, openly plotting to overthrow successful revolutionary governments, and supporting surrogate counter-revolutionary forces in countries throughout the globe. National political traditions, however, are not cut of whole cloth but rather contain sometimes surprising divergences and contradictions. The present anti-revolutionary vocation of the United States, in fact, makes it all the more interesting to find the thought of a revolutionary such as Jefferson at its core. When reading some of Jefferson's most radical writings, then, it is hard not to be struck by the vast gulf that separates his thinking from that of the current United States, its ideology, its constitution, and its political system and culture.

After this initial surprise at the fact that Jefferson's thought belongs to the revolutionary tradition, we should recognize how it still has important contributions to make, and can help us move beyond some of the central obstacles to thinking about revolution today. Jefferson's declarations of independence throughout his life not only mark the separation of the colonies from the colonial power but also, and more importantly, seek to keep alive the pursuit of freedom within society – striving to conceive of how the revolutionary process can continue indefinitely, how what eighteenth-century revolutionaries called "public happiness" can be instituted in government, and ultimately how self-rule and democracy can be realized.

In my view, the approach that allows us best to see what Jefferson has to contribute to contemporary revolutionary thought focuses on his concept of revolutionary transition. Like all great revolutionary thinkers, Jefferson understands well that the revolutionary event, the rupture with the past and the destruction of the old regime, is not the end of the revolution but really only a beginning. The event opens a period of transition that aims at realizing the goals of the revolution. The concept of transition, however, is today a fundamental stumbling block of revolutionary thought and practice. The (often authoritarian) means employed during revolutionary transitions frequently conflict with and even contradict the desired (democratic) ends; moreover, these transitions never seem to come to an end. The travelers on the long journey through the desert end up getting completely lost, no nearer to the promised land, and that leader with a big stick starts looking a lot like the old Pharaoh. In fact, whenever revolutionaries start talking to you about "transition" today, you had better watch out: they are probably trying to put one over on you. Jefferson's thought, however, poses a novel conception of transition, which can help steer revolutionary thought around its current obstacles. He provocatively brings together, on the one hand, constitution and rebellion and, on the other, transition and democracy. In other words, for Jefferson the work of the revolution must continue incessantly, periodically reopening the constituent process, and the population must be trained in democracy through the practices of democracy.

Before moving on to what is revolutionary in Jefferson's thought I should point out some difficulties of reading him in this context. Jefferson is not a systematic thinker and, although his complete works fill dozens of large volumes, he left no extended treatises or even essays on politics. The vast majority of his writings, and the most interesting ones, consist of his correspondence with friends and public figures. His letters are most often centered on contemporary events, using them as the point of departure for more general political and philosophical reflection. In addition, the letters are frequently crafted for a specific addressee: to John Adams, for instance, he expresses much more moderate views than he does to James Madison. The letters thus require a different method of reading than do traditional texts of political theory, moving from the specific occasion to general discussions.

Furthermore, Jefferson not infrequently contradicts himself in both his writings and his actions as a politician. Reading his work therefore requires a stringent process of selection that identifies and brings together a coherent set of interesting ideas. The point, of course, is not to give a balanced picture of Jefferson's thought as a whole, even if that were actually possible in the case of such a far-reaching and unsystematic thinker. And so this collection of texts is not aimed at being representative – indeed one could easily choose texts that would give an entirely different view. The point of this volume, instead, is to discover and learn from what remains revolutionary in Jefferson's thought.

Finally, one should always keep in mind, even while appreciating what Jefferson has to offer the revolutionary tradition, the reactionary elements of his political thought and practice. For this reason I have included at the end of this anthology a selection of Jefferson's writings on race, regarding black slaves and Native Americans. These texts can help the reader recognize not only Jefferson's racist views but also his racist actions, both as slaveholder and as a central figure, in many respects, of the destruction of Native American lands and cultures. It would be a useful and fascinating project to explore how Jefferson's inability to think about equality with respect to race corresponds to the continuing forms of racial inequality in US society and culture today, but that, clearly, is outside the scope of this book. For our purposes, reading such texts can serve, at the very least, as a healthy guard against any uncritical celebration of Jefferson.

TRANSITION AS SOLUTION AND PROBLEM

Before exploring Jefferson's notion of transition we have first to outline the concept's function and the difficulties it presents in the modern revolutionary tradition. It is Lenin who poses the role of transition with the greatest clarity and realism, and his analysis has effectively framed all subsequent discussions on the topic. For Lenin, the process of transition solves a central conundrum of revolution: the role of state power and democratic rule after the revolutionary event. On one side, he situates himself against the opportunists and social democrats who claim that the state apparatus must be maintained permanently, serving as an organ to reconcile the classes. The state, Lenin counters, is always an instrument of oppression and it stands in the way of the revolutionary goal to create a new, fuller democracy: no longer "a democracy for the minority, only for the possessing classes, only for the rich," but rather a "democracy for the poor, democracy for the people."[1] The democracy Lenin has in mind is one in which people are able to rule themselves actively and collectively, managing the economy, organizing political exchange, and resolving social conflicts with no power standing above them. In the interests of democracy, then, the state must be abolished. On the other side, Lenin situates himself against the anarchists who propose the abolition of the state at a single stroke, on Day One of the revolution, which act they claim will allow people to rule themselves democratically. Thinking primarily in military terms, Lenin first of all objects that the repressive state apparatus is temporarily necessary in order to protect the revolution against its enemies. His second and more profoundly political objection is that the anarchists fail to recognize the real condition of the population and, specifically, the lack of the capacities necessary for self-rule and democracy. We need to understand how to make a revolution, he insists, "with human nature as it is now, with human nature that cannot do without subordination, control, and 'managers'."[2] There is no point in dreaming of the politics of an ideal population – this is one of Lenin's many Machiavellian moments – rather, we must think politics in terms of the real, present circumstances.

Lenin thus poses as his solution, as if between the two inadequate views – the social-democratic preservation of the state and the anarchist immediate abolition of it – a process of transition. The revolution will be realized over time. The state apparatus is not immediately abolished but withers away. Similarly, a dictatorship of the proletariat replaces bourgeois dictatorship and defers democracy, which will arrive only when the transition is complete. Lenin's argument here is focused on the temporality of the revolutionary event. On the one side, in the social-democratic view, the revolutionary event never actually takes place and there is instead only a continuous duration of reform without rupture. For the anarchists, on the other side, the revolutionary event is punctual and absolute, assuming that everything can change overnight. Lenin instead conceives the revolutionary event as both rupture and duration, an historical break that opens a new historical process.

The key to Lenin's thought here, and the point that will bring us to Jefferson, is the process necessary to transform human nature, the process that allows the multitude to develop the capacities for self-rule. The real mistake of the social democrats is that they assume that the multitude is not and never will be capable of democracy, that human nature requires a division between the rulers and the ruled, and hence that state power must be maintained. The mistake of the anarchists is that they assume the multitude is already capable of democracy, as if the capacities for self-rule were part of human nature and will spontaneously spring to life fully formed once the repressive apparatuses of class rule are removed. What neither the social democrats nor the anarchists understand is that human nature can and must be transformed. Human nature as it is now, which, as Lenin says, has been formed by subordination, must be made anew. The capacities necessary for democracy and self-rule, in other words, can and must be learned; they require education and training. Over time, Lenin explains, "observing the simple, fundamental rules of every-day social life in common will have become a *habit*."[3] The revolutionary transition for Lenin is thus a period of education and training in which the multitude learns how to rule itself, in which democracy becomes an ingrained characteristic.

Looking back today on Lenin's proposal for a revolutionary transition, written on the eve of the October Revolution, it is easy to use subsequent historical developments to disqualify it. One might say, for instance, that the history of the Soviet Union demonstrates that transitions never end, that the state does not wither away but merely takes a new form. That type of historical reasoning, however, is unsatisfactory for evaluating a conceptual argument. It is much more useful, instead, to focus on the concepts themselves. From this perspective, the weakest element of Lenin's notion of transition – one which indeed might figure in an account of some of the tragedies of the Soviet experience – lies in the radical division it requires between means and ends, between the form of transitional rule and the revolutionary goals. This is the point on which Jefferson will help us take a step beyond the impasse of revolutionary thought.

REBELLION AGAINST THE GOVERNMENT

The first key to understanding Jefferson's notion of transition is to recognize the continuous and dynamic relationship he poses between rebellion and constitution or, rather, between revolution and government. A conventional view of revolution conceives these terms in temporal sequence: rebellion is necessary to overthrow the old regime, but when it falls and the new government is formed, rebellion must cease. In other words, the constituent power of the revolution must yield to the newly constituted power. In contrast to this view, Jefferson insists on the virtue and necessity of periodic rebellion – even against the newly formed government. The processes of constituent power, he says, must continually disrupt and force open an establishment of constituted power.[4]

Jefferson celebrates the virtues of revolt against the government most clearly and radically in his letters about Shays' Rebellion. In the summer of 1786, while Jefferson is serving as US minister to France, a mere decade after the War of Independence breaks out, and only three years after the peace treaty with Britain is signed, a court in western Massachusetts rules to imprison farmers who cannot pay their debts, seizing their land and property. The farmers, many of whom are veterans of the Revolutionary War – including Daniel Shays, their leader – organize an armed resistance to block the courts, protect their property, and free their imprisoned comrades from jail. In the course of a year the rebels are defeated and hunted down, their leaders executed.

Shays' Rebellion holds a position in US history somewhat analogous to that of the 1921 Kronstadt rebellion in Soviet history. Although that later event was on a much larger and bloodier scale, as well as embroiled in questions of international conspiracy, both rebellions involved veterans of revolutionary war challenging the new governments on economic agricultural issues; both were perceived by the newly formed governments as serious threats, and both were violently suppressed.

One might imagine that Abigail Adams' reaction to the events would be representative of those of the majority of Jefferson's colleagues who had struggled to form the new government and were involved at the time in debates about the Constitution. "Ignorant, wrestless desperadoes, without conscience or principals," she writes in a letter to Jefferson, "have led a deluded multitude to follow their standard, under pretence of grievances which have no existence but in their imaginations."[5] Jefferson, however, feels no such indignation at the actions of the rebels but rather celebrates them. "The spirit of resistance to government," he responds to Abigail Adams, "is so valuable on certain occasions, that I wish it to be always kept alive. It will often be exercised when wrong, but better so than not to be exercised at all. I like a little rebellion now and then. It is like a storm in the Atmosphere."[6] Rebellion against the government, he maintains, is so virtuous that it should not only be tolerated but even encouraged.

One remarkable element of Jefferson's view on these events is that he does not support the rebels simply because their cause is just. The news he receives in Paris, in any case, is probably insufficient to judge adequately the situation in Massachusetts, but he assumes the rebels' motives are mistaken. "The people cannot be all, & always, well informed," he writes to William Short, continuing a theme from his letter to Abigail Adams, but their ignorance does not negate the virtue of their rebellion. "If they remain quiet under such misconceptions," he continues, "it is a lethargy, the forerunner of death to the public liberty."[7] Jefferson's support even for actions based on ignorance and misconceptions makes his point about the necessity of continuing rebellion all the more strongly. Rebellion is not just a matter of correcting wrongs committed by the government, and thus only valuable if its cause is just; rebellion has an intrinsic value, regardless of the justness of its specific grievances and goals. Periodic rebellion is necessary to guarantee the health of a society and preserve public freedom. "God forbid we should ever be 20 years without such a rebellion," he writes. In Jefferson's view, rebellion should not become our constant condition; rather, it should eternally return.

Just in case Jefferson's reader might think his conception of rebellion too innocent, even angelic, he adds a few lines in his letter to Short to emphasize its brutality and violence. Jefferson is perfectly aware that rebellions are bloody but he easily accepts the sacrifice of a few lives when freedom is at stake. "The tree of liberty must be refreshed from time to time with the blood of patriots & tyrants. It is it's [*sic*] natural manure."[8] The language of patriots and tyrants recalls the heroic rhetoric of the previous decade and the War of Independence. Back then the patriots were the rebellious colonists and the tyrant the English king. Now, however, in the context of Shays' Rebellion, Jefferson casts the rebellious indebted farmers in the role of patriots and the new government in the position of tyrant. The roles have changed, but the principle remains the same. That the United States has achieved independence does not diminish the virtue of rebellion against its government.

Jefferson endorses the need for violence even more strongly when writing in support of the French Revolution. In the bloody year of 1793, after returning to the United States, Jefferson writes in support of the Jacobins to William Short, who has taken over his position as emissary in France. In the course of the revolution many guilty people have been killed by "the arm of the people" and also some innocents have died, but this is, in his view, a small price to pay. "The liberty of the whole earth was depending on the issue of the contest, and was ever such a prize won with so little innocent blood? My own affections have been deeply wounded by some of the martyrs to this cause, but rather than it should have failed, I would have seen half the earth desolated. Were there but an Adam & Eve left in every country, & left free, it would be better than as it now is."[9] Jefferson is not bashful about accepting bloodshed for the cause of freedom. This is true in the case of both rebellion and revolution, and it is striking, in fact, how similarly Jefferson writes about the two events.

This virtue of a continual return of rebellion, finally, corresponds in Jefferson's thought with the need for a periodic reopening of the constituent process. Too many people look on formal constitutions with sanctimonious reverence, he explains, and consider them immutable. Clearly he does not believe that future generations should be bound to the intentions of the original framers of the constitution. "We might as well require a man to wear still the coat that fitted him when a boy."[10] The dead are nothing, he declares. The earth belongs to the living. "Every constitution, then, and every law, naturally expires at the end of 19 years. If it be enforced longer, it is an act of force and not of right."[11] Thus, every twenty years, which Jefferson calculates to be the turnover time of a generation, a new constituent process must therefore throw off the dead weight of the past and write a constitution based on the desires and needs of the new generation.

I think it no coincidence that Jefferson proposes in very similar terms the eternal return at twenty-year intervals of these two events: rebellion against the government and the revision of the constitution. They are, in effect, two faces of the same event, the one blood-spattered and the other relatively peaceful. A society cannot be allowed to close around a constituted power but must periodically be opened up to a new constituent process. Whether blood must be spilled or not depends on circumstances, but the essential for Jefferson is that freedom be maintained and that the project of the revolution continue.

TRANSITION AND DEMOCRACY

By bringing together rebellion and constitution Jefferson formulates a notion of revolutionary transition as something like permanent revolution or, more precisely, as the periodic renovation of the revolution. This transition never ends; in fact, Jefferson insists it must always be kept alive. Does that mean that the revolutionary process is continually frustrated, never able to reach its goal? No, because for Jefferson the transition has a clear direction but no endpoint. What we need to understand here – and this is perhaps the most important Jeffersonian insight for contemporary revolutionary theory – is that the means and ends of the transition are never separated entirely: democracy is the goal of the revolutionary process and, paradoxically, democracy is also the means of achieving it.

We should note, of course, that Jefferson does not use the term *democracy* – it was seldom used in a positive sense by revolutionaries of the period – but his thought does contain a strong concept of democracy that corresponds to some of the more radical contemporary uses of the term. In Jefferson we can often read democracy when he uses the term *republicanism*. "Were I to assign to this term a precise and definite idea," he writes about the term *republic*, "I would say, purely and simply, it means a government by its citizens in mass, acting directly and personally, according to rules established by the majority; and that every other government is more or less republican, in proportion as it has in its composition more or less of this ingredient of the direct action of the citizens."[12] Jefferson's insistence, in particular, on the direct action of the population in government – not through representatives determined by election or otherwise – is one element that makes this a radically democratic conception. Our present task, then, is to understand how such a democratic government constituted by the direct and active participation of citizens can be both the goal of the revolutionary transition and the means of achieving it.

We saw earlier, together with Lenin, that "human nature as it is now," trained to be subservient and passive, is not capable of democracy. It has the wrong habits. Or we might say, along with Spinoza, that if the population is ignorant and superstitious then establishing democracy would merely mean instituting the rule of ignorance and superstition. The multitude will not be spontaneously or immediately transformed by the revolutionary event. It is the role of the transition to accomplish this task: to make a multitude capable of democracy, with the skills, talents, and knowledges necessary to rule themselves. This is the primary challenge for revolutionary thought, the stumbling block that, unless negotiated successfully, will bring down any theory.

Before proceeding with our analysis of Jefferson's thought, therefore, it is useful to examine how some of the most innovative and influential present-day theorists confront this same point. Slavoj Žižek is one of the very few contemporary thinkers whose theoretical arsenal is rich enough to be able to confront the question of revolution and articulate how it can be conceived today. The central element in Žižek's provocation to "return to Lenin" in recent years, in fact, might be summed up in the need for a revolutionary transition that can transform the people, and thus confront the very problem we are considering here. "[W]e should bravely admit that it is in fact a duty — even *the* duty — of a revolutionary party to 'dissolve the people and elect another,'" he writes, ironically citing a poem by Brecht, "that is, to bring about the transubstantiation of the 'old' opportunistic people (the inert 'crowd') into a revolutionary body aware of its historical task, to transform the body of the empirical people into a body of Truth."[13] One of the great merits of Žižek's work is to insist so strongly and clearly on the need for this transformation and to criticize those who fail to face this challenge, counting naively on the spontaneous virtue, wisdom, and goodness of the people. The first difficulty with his proposition, however — and here he is indeed following Lenin — is that the source of the transformation comes from above, from outside the people. The form of authority that is to lead this operation is radically different from, and perhaps even in contradiction to, the new, fuller democracy that Lenin sees as its goal (although it is less clear that Žižek shares with Lenin the goal of democracy). The second problem, which perhaps follows from the first, is that Žižek proposes no mechanism for achieving this transformation. He refers to the notion of transubstantiation in this passage perhaps to emphasize how drastically the social body must be transformed, but the formulation also implies that the operation is not a continuous becoming; rather, it involves a radical leap the logic of which is mysterious, perhaps even mystical.

Ernesto Laclau has made equally extensive and valuable contributions to radical thought and, despite the constant criticisms between the two, on the specific point that we are considering here his view and Žižek's are very close. It is difficult to do justice to the complexity of Laclau's thought without adopting his highly developed and precise vocabulary in its entirety, but we can nonetheless indicate the point in his thinking that corresponds to the problem we are discussing. Laclau considers democratic politics to be the endpoint of an extended logical sequence beginning with his assertion that the social field is radically heterogeneous and has no spontaneous or pregiven order. The logical process leading to politics and ultimately to democracy begins, for Laclau, with the specific demands that arise on this social field – demands for bread, for instance, or for rights or services or freedoms. Correspondences among these demands must be recognized so that they can be articulated together and form a chain of equivalents. That chain of equivalents must be given coherence such that out of the plurality of demands is constructed a popular identity – that is, such that the "the people" is produced. And, finally, the production of the people is the necessary condition for democracy. The essential issue for Laclau, then, is to identify the motor that drives this sequence because, like Žižek, he insists that the creation of the people is not spontaneous: "nothing in those demands, individually considered, announces a 'manifest destiny' by which they should tend to coalesce into a kind of unity – nothing in them anticipates that they should constitute a chain."[14] And a chain of equivalents similarly does not immediately or spontaneously create the people. What is necessary, Laclau insists, is a hegemonic figure that stands above the social field and from that transcendent position is able to guide this process, articulating the individual elements, posing a unity, and thereby creating the people. Laclau takes great pains to insist that this is not a fully fledged transcendence but a "failed transcendence" that nonetheless is able to fulfill the role of hegemony; and similarly, the hegemonic figure is not necessarily the party but it nonetheless fills the party function.

It seems, then, that if we are not to believe naively that the multitude will be immediately and spontaneously transformed after the revolutionary event, and thus fall into the error that Lenin attributes to the anarchists, we are forced to accept with Žižek and Laclau that the population must be transformed by a figure of authority or hegemony that stands above it. The problem, once again, is the separation between means and ends in this view: the undemocratic, hegemonic process of transition that is meant to result eventually in democracy. And here we return to Jefferson because, although he too recognizes that the multitude as it exists now must be transformed, he conceives of the process that leads to democracy as proceeding through a kind of democratic training.

Like many other revolutionary theorists, most notably, perhaps, Mao and Gramsci, Jefferson devotes considerable attention to popular education. Schools and libraries are indeed relevant to this discussion because they are essential for the creation of the new habits, skills, and knowledges that can sustain democratic self-government. What most clearly reveals the essence of Jefferson's notion of revolutionary transition, though, is his proposal in the second decade of the nineteenth century for a system of wards or "little republics," as an experiment in local autonomy. In these years, Jefferson repeatedly criticizes the lack of democracy in US political life and its constitution. Since, as we saw earlier, his standard for republicanism is the active and direct participation of citizens and their control over the organs of power, he charges that the United States is much less republican than ought to be expected.[15] Forty years after the War of Independence, the revolutionary process has stalled, fallen back on itself, become closed in a constituted power. Jefferson's idea to reopen the revolutionary process is to divide each county into wards of such a size that every citizen can participate in political deliberations actively and in person. These little republics would have full autonomy to decide all local issues, controlling issues of justice, police, public welfare, and so forth. Furthermore, Jefferson proposes that the wards send delegates to compose the next highest body of government, the county, which in turn would send delegates to the state level, which, finally, would send delegates to the national government.

It is striking how strongly this schema resembles the institutions established by the Paris Commune some fifty years later.[16] Marx himself admires in the Commune exactly the elements that Jefferson proposes in the ward schema: active participation, local autonomy, and a pyramid of delegation. Both Marx and Jefferson see this participatory government as an antidote to the dominant, undemocratic form of parliamentary representation. "Instead of deciding once in three or six years which member of the ruling class was to misrepresent the people in Parliament," Marx writes, the measures of the Commune "betoken the tendency of a government of the people by the people."[17] Jefferson anticipates Marx's words and adds that the experience of participation in government transforms people: "Where every man is a sharer in the direction of his ward–republic, or of some of the higher ones, and feels that he is a participator in the government of affairs, not merely at an election one day in the year, but every day; when there shall not be a man in the State who will not be a member of some one of its councils, great or small, he will let the heart be torn out of his body sooner than his power be wrested from him by a Caesar or a Bonaparte."[18] Participatory self-rule not only stands opposed to the current sham of democracy that merely legitimates authority through electoral mechanisms, in Jefferson's view it also – and more importantly – creates people who will fight against any form of authority that tries to take power from them. Marx is perhaps referring to a similar transformative process when he suggests in the passage above that the structures of the Commune indicate a "tendency" toward democratic government.

The most important aspect of participatory democracy is how it changes people. It serves as an educational experience, training the multitude in the skills and capacities it needs to rule itself. We should be clear that Jefferson is not repeating the error that Lenin criticized of those who naively believe that a new democracy will emerge spontaneously on the basis of human nature as it is now. Along with Lenin (and, in different ways, Žižek and Laclau), Jefferson recognizes that people must be transformed, that a new people must be created. Reflecting on the South American independence movements in the 1820s, for example, he acknowledges that "the qualifications for self-government in society are not innate. They are the result of habit and long training, and for these they will require time and probably much suffering."[19] Creating a new human nature, for Jefferson as for Lenin, is a matter of training and habits. This new humanity is not the prerequisite on which the revolution takes place, but rather the *outcome* of the revolutionary process. "I have no fear but that the result of our experiment will be," Jefferson writes with respect to Shays'

Rebellion, "that men may be trusted to govern themselves without a master."[20] This lengthy process necessary to create a multitude able to govern itself without a master – a painful and often bloody process – returns us squarely to the theme of transition.

The crucial difference in Jefferson's thought, though, is that the means to accomplish the transition are not separate from its ends. The schema of autonomy and democratic participation, such as the ward system or the Paris Commune, is not the end of the revolutionary transition but rather its primary means. People are transformed by practicing autonomy and participating in government. From this perspective it makes no sense for the transition to be ruled over by a hegemonic figure, whether that be a dictatorship of the proletariat or any other force that stands above or transcends the multitude. How could democracy, after all, result from its opposite? A transition ruled by a hegemonic figure does not teach people anything about self-rule; it only reinforces their habits of subservience and passivity. People only learn democracy by doing it. The necessary transformation – learning to rule ourselves without a master – can only take place through practice, in action. One might object at this point that such a concept of transition is paradoxical insofar as it collapses means and ends; pretending to achieve democracy through democracy it merely stands in place. To resolve this paradox we simply have to recognize that means and ends are not identical here but neither are they entirely separate. The democracy aimed for always exceeds the democracy practiced, and thus the transition is recast as a process of infinite becoming.

We should dwell a bit longer on how Jefferson's notion of transition undermines arguments for hegemony. We are no longer bound to the choice of either trusting in the spontaneous capacities of people as they are now or accepting the rule of a hegemonic power charged with the task of creating a new people. Instead, between these two or, really, outside of this false alternative, Jefferson declares that when people participate actively in government, deciding on all the matters that concern them, either directly or by instructing their delegates up to the highest levels of government, they are transformed. There is no great instructor that teaches them the necessary lessons. The process of transition is a self-training in the capacities of self-rule. Through practice they develop the skills, knowledges, and habits necessary for self-government and, in the process, a new humanity is created. Those formed in this process can be trusted, as Jefferson says, to rule themselves without a master and, in fact, will attack violently any potential master who tries to usurp their power. They will defend the revolution against its enemies, against any Caesar or Bonaparte.

FROM REBELLION TO DEMOCRACY

As we have seen, Jefferson radically alters the traditional concept of transition by bringing together constitution and rebellion, on the one hand, and on the other transition and democracy. It might be more accurate, though, to say that in this way Jefferson does away entirely with the concept of transition, because each of these two conceptual operations poses a new temporality of the revolutionary event. No longer is there a beginning and an end, which a concept of transition would require; rather there is a repeated event and an unending revolutionary process of becoming.

The first conceptual operation, bringing together constitution and rebellion, poses the time of revolution as a periodic repetition. The revolutionary event, therefore, does not just happen once. Each generation must keep the spirit of revolution alive by rebelling against the government, revising the constitution, and reopening the constituent process. The only way to be faithful to the revolution, in other words, is to repeat it. The temporal figure of the revolutionary event, therefore, is the eternal return – not the return of the same, of course, but the return of the different, that is, the difference marked by each generation.

The second conceptual operation, which poses democracy as both means and end, even more dramatically undermines the traditional concept of transition. This relationship between means and end is, in fact, something like an expanding spiral. The democracy aimed for always exceeds the democracy practiced, such that as the democracy practiced expands through the process of self-training, so too expands the democracy aimed for, the horizon of self-rule. Training in practice, in other words, constantly nourishes too the powers of political imagination and desire. So, the real revolutionary event from this perspective is the progressive transformation of humanity, the constant democratic self-making of the multitude. This event is not a one-time affair, but an incessant process of becoming.

What is most important about Jefferson's conception of the revolutionary process, however, is not its temporal figure but its substance. The real core revolutionary event is the metamorphosis of the multitude, its developing the new skills, knowledges, and habits necessary to rule itself without masters, along with the expansion of its imagination and desire for democracy. This revolutionary event is not a contentless abyss and it does not come from the outside; it is an immanent process, a learning of democracy by doing it, a self-transformation.

AND FROM DEMOCRACY TO REBELLION

Focusing on democracy in this way should not make us forget Jefferson's insistence on rebellion for the health of society. One should not assume, in other words, that once some democratic process is in place rebellion against the government is no longer necessary and desirable. Jefferson, of course, advocates rebellion against tyranny in all its forms, but he does not call for rebellion only when things go badly. He does not even require that a rebellion be based on just causes in order to be virtuous. The constant becoming of the revolutionary process must be punctuated periodically with (often bloody) ruptures. Jefferson's revolutionary thought thus moves back and forth between these two poles: from rebellion to democracy and from democracy to rebellion.

Why would Jefferson advocate periodic rebellion even when the revolution has inaugurated a democratic process? One response is that over time the revolution process tends to fall back on itself – whether at the hands of internal and external enemies or simply through corruption and exhaustion – and thus periodic rebellion is a way to remain faithful to the revolutionary event, restoring it. Another response is that even when a democratic process moves forward it reaches thresholds that cannot be crossed without the rupture provided by rebellion. New tyrannies arise or are newly made visible that block the process of democratic reform. (It is unlikely, for instance, that Jefferson's ward system could have been instituted in the early nineteenth century without some act of force.) Both of these responses are correct, but they do not yet touch the heart of the matter.

The dynamic between democracy and rebellion has to be understood in terms of Jefferson's notion of transforming human nature, his constitutive ontology. In this context we can see how absurd are all those debates about humans being naturally good or naturally evil. (They are, by the way, neither.) The relevant fact for politics is that human nature is susceptible to change, that humans can become different. This is how, as we saw earlier, Jefferson's dedication to education is central to his revolutionary thought. The revolutionary process requires a remaking of human nature that destroys the habits of servitude and develops the capacities for self-rule. Along with these capacities grow the political imagination and desires, which can press continually far beyond the present political situation. Satisfaction with the current regime is a sign not of political health in Jefferson's view but of lethargy, the beginnings of the death of public liberty. Rebellion is how each generation throws off the old and new forms of tyranny it faces, how it expresses the disjunction between its political desires and its political reality, imposing a rupture that sets off a new "educational" cycle of transforming human nature.

This continual relay from rebellion to democratic process and back again strikingly marks the discord between Jefferson's revolutionary thought and the history of the United States. Numerous heroic efforts to rebel against the US government and various projects for local autonomy and democratic participation have indeed been launched, but their successes and frequency pale in comparison to what Jefferson imagined.[21] The prestige of Jefferson in the US canon might serve to renew such discussions and to open spaces for participation and rebellion.

In our day, however, we can no longer consider this dynamic only in a national framework, as Jefferson did, but must try to understand it in the global terrain, a context that obviously brings enormous challenges but also some surprising opportunities. We have to imagine what structures of local autonomy and democratic participation today can serve to train the multitude in the necessary capacities for self-rule and, moreover, rekindle the desire for and imagination of a new, full democracy. We have to discover what forms of rebellion can assault and successfully transform the global imperial order in a way that opens new constituent democratic processes. And in order to accomplish this we should look first at how people around the world are already putting into practice forms of democratic participation and rebellion.

All of this requires us to go well beyond anything that Jefferson offers. His revolutionary thought, however, does give us the terms for thinking revolutionary transition today, between democracy and rebellion, and imposes on us a rigorous schedule – at least every twenty years. By my calculation we are well overdue.

NOTES

I would like to thank Barry Shank for his generous assistance in preparing this volume. He gave suggestions on the selection of texts and has been a tireless and inspiring conversation partner on topics relating to Jefferson and democracy in the US context.

1   V.I. Lenin, *State and Revolution*, New York: International Publishers 1971, pp. 72–3. All further references to Lenin are from this edition.
2   Ibid., p. 43.
3   Ibid., p. 85.
4   On the concept and history of constituent power, see Antonio Negri, *Insurgencies*, Minneapolis: University of Minnesota Press 1999.
5   See below, p. 28.
6   See below, p. 30.
7   See below, p. 35.
8   See below, p. 35.
9   See below, p. 47.
10   See below, p. 73.
11   See below, p. 57.
12   See below, p. 65.
13   Slavoj Žižek, *The Parallax View*, Cambridge (MA): MIT Press 2006, p. 149.
14   Ernesto Laclau, *On Populist Reason*, London and New York: Verso 2005, p. 162.
15   See below, p66–7.
16   Hannah Arendt notes the similarities between Jefferson's ward proposal and the Paris Commune, along with the system of Russian soviets and German communist councils. See *On Revolution*, New York: Viking 1963, pp. 248–50 and 256–58. One important difference, of course, is that Jefferson does not recognize as clearly the class nature of such a political project.
17   Karl Marx, *Civil War in France: The Paris Commune*, New York: International Publishers 1988, pp. 59, 65.
18   See below, p. 63.
19   "Jefferson to Edward Everett, March 27, 1824," in Jefferson, *Writings*, Volume 16, Andrew Lipscomb, ed., Washington (DC): Thomas Jefferson Memorial Association 1904, p. 22.

[20] See below, p. 32.

[21] W.E.B. Du Bois, who in many ways is the rightful heir to Jefferson's thought in the US tradition, gives us one example of such a relay between rebellion and democracy in his account of the "general strike" of plantation slaves during the Civil War and the democratic process guided by Freedman's Bureau in the post-war period. See *Black Reconstruction*, New York: Russell & Russell 1935.

SELECTED
FURTHER READING

SELECTED TEXTS BY JEFFERSON

All known correspondence written by Jefferson in chronological order:

The Papers of Thomas Jefferson edited by Julian Boyd, et al. Princeton, NJ,
   Princeton University Press, 1950 – . (33 volumes at date of this publication,
   ongoing)

Accurate single volume edition of Jefferson's major writings and letters:

*Thomas Jefferson: Writings: Autobiography, Notes on the State of Virginia, Public
   and Private Papers, Addresses, Letters*, edited by Merrill D. Peterson, New
   York, NY, Library of America, 1984.

Other editions of Jefferson's writings:

Jefferson's Extracts from the Gospels, edited by Dickinson W. Adams,
Princeton, NJ, Princeton University Press, 1983.
Notes on the State of Virginia, edited by William Peden, Chapel Hill, NC,
   University of North Carolina Press, 1954.
The Adams-Jefferson Letters, edited by Lester J. Cappon, Chapel Hill, NC,
   University of North Carolina Press, 1959.
*The Republic of Letters: The Correspondence between Thomas Jefferson and James
   Madison*, edited by James Morton Smith, New York, NY, Norton, 1995.
Thomas Jefferson, Political Writings, edited by Joyce Appleby and Terence Ball,
   Cambridge, Cambridge University Press, 1999.

SELECTED TEXTS ON JEFFERSON

BIOGRAPHY

MALONE, Dumas, *Jefferson and His Time* (six volumes), Boston, MA, Little, Brown, 1948–81.

PETERSON, Merrill D., *Thomas Jefferson and the New Nation: A Biography*, Oxford, Oxford University Press, 1970.

On Jefferson's Thought

KOCH, Adrienne, *The Philosophy of Thomas Jefferson*, New York, Columbia University Press, 1943.

ONUF, Peter S., *The Mind of Thomas Jefferson*, Charlottesville, VA, University of Virginia Press, 2007.

Commentaries on Radicalism, Democracy, and the American Revolution

APPLEBY, Joyce, *Capitalism and a New Social Order: The Republican Vision of the 1790s*, New York, NY, New York University Press, 1984.

ARENDT, Hannah, *On Revolution*, New York, NY, Viking, 1963.

MATTHEWS, Richard K., *The Radical Politics of Thomas Jefferson: A Revisionist View*, Lawrence, KS, Kansas University Press, 1984.

NEGRI, Antonio, *Insurgencies: Constituent Power and the Modern State*, translated by Maurizia Boscagli, Minneapolis, MN, University of Minnesota Press, 1999.

WOOD, Gordon, *Radicalism of the American Revolution*, New York, NY, A. A. Knopf, 1992.

Selected Online resources:

Thomas Jefferson Digital Archive at the University of Virginia Library:
   http://etext.lib.virginia.edu/jefferson/
70,000 original documents may be found as JPEG files online:
Thomas Jefferson Papers at the Library of Congress:
   http://memory.loc.gov/ ammem/collections/jefferson_papers/

GLOSSARY OF NAMES

Adams, Abigail (1744–1818): wife and partner of John Adams, second president of the United States. As the Revolutionary War raged, she wrote engaged, politically lively letters to the future second president for which she is now famous. They were not, however, solely limited to the affairs of her husband: at one point she encouraged him to "remember the ladies" when forming the new government of the United States.

Banneker, Benjamin (1731–1806): as son of a freed African slave, Banneker was self-educated in advanced levels of literature, mathematics, and history. He was an accomplished mathematician, astronomer, and publisher of *Banneker's Almanac*, which Banneker delivered to Jefferson as a demonstration of African-American intellectual achievement. The accompanying letter sparked a published debate with Jefferson on the abolition of slavery and racial equality.

Breckenridge, John (1760–1806): lawyer and US Senator (Kentucky) who traveled Europe extensively in his youth. During Jefferson's presidency, Breckenridge was a close political ally who often proposed bills allegedly authored by the president. In turn, Jefferson appointed Breckenridge US Attorney General during his second term, a seat that he held until his death the following year.

Cabell, Joseph C. (1778–1856): Virginia politician whose political ambitions never rose above the state level. Jefferson recruited Cabell in 1815 to anchor the public university initiative spawned by his "Bill for the More General Diffusion of Knowledge" (1779). Cabell remained an active university fundraiser and advocate in the Virginia legislature for decades after the university opened to students.

Carrington, Edward (1748–1810): Virginia delegate to the Continental Congress who served as lieutenant colonel in the Continental Army, fighting in the battles of Hobkirk's Hill and Yorktown. Carrington consulted his close friend, George Washington, on matters of Virginia politics and was appointed to several crucial diplomatic roles negotiating with the British on behalf of the newly formed US government.

Chastellux, Marquis de; François Jean de Beauvoir (1734–1788): French political ally and close friend to Jefferson in Paris. Their friendship began while Chastellux served in the American Revolution.

Coles, Edward (1786–1868): born in Virginia to wealthy plantation owners, Coles inherited his family's estate at age 23. Coles became an ardent advocate for abolition after studying Enlightenment philosophy at the College of William and Mary. Legally unable to free his slaves in Virginia, Coles moved westward freeing them en route. The thankful freedmen followed him to Illinois where he provided each with his own farm. Unbeknownst to Coles, the Illinois legislature was busy revising its constitutional provision toward legalizing slavery. Coles promptly declared gubernatorial candidacy, winning by a subtle margin. As governor, he fought tirelessly throughout his tenure to revise the Illinois Black Codes.

Diodati-Tronchin (de Genève), Jean, Comte de: Swiss count and minister plenipotentiary of the Duke of Mecklenburg-Schwerin. The Comte and Comtesse (Marie Élizabeth) entertained Jefferson during his diplomatic stay in Paris where they socialized extensively. He and Jefferson exchanged communiqués regarding the US and France's mutually nascent governments.

Handsome Lake [Ganioda'yo] (c. 1735–1815): spiritual leader, prophet, and chief of the Seneca Nation (Iroquois League) whose teachings forbade alcoholic consumption, adultery, and other amoral behavior. Thought by many to have hybridized Christian and indigenous social values after a vision of the Great Spirit, Ganioda'yo organized a new religion, Gui'wiio (Good Message). He fought against the Americans in the Revolutionary War, but later encouraged his followers to reconcile with the new government and to acculturate to reservation life. He traveled to Washington to discuss the fair trade of native territories with Thomas Jefferson in 1802.

Hartley, David (1732–1813): British Member of Parliament who argued relentlessly against the institution of slavery, declaring it "contrary to the laws of God and the rights of man." Hartley was also amongst the first in British government to call for the reconciliation with the newly independent United States. After signing the Treaty of Paris (1783), he worked to open commercial relations between Great Britain and its former colonies.

Harrison, William Henry (1773–1841): as governor of the American Northwest Territory, Harrison brokered land purchases from Native Americans, making available large swaths of land for white settlement in present-day Illinois, Indiana, Michigan, Wisconsin, and Minnesota. Harrison's command of the Army of the Northwest (AN) was pivotal in territorial battles against indigenous tribes – one of which was notably led by Tecumseh, who was killed in battle by the AN in 1813. Harrison was elected President of the United States in 1840 but died in office 30 days later.

Hawkins, Benjamin (1754–1816): as General Superintendent of Indian Affairs, Hawkins oversaw relations with Native American tribes south of the Ohio Valley, maintaining peaceful associations with the Creek, Cherokee, Choctaw, and Chickasaw for over two decades. As chief negotiator and administrator of this region, Hawkins often advised presidents on bureaucratic relations between the American government and Indian leadership. Peace was largely maintained until the Red Sticks, a faction of the Creek and led by Tecumseh, attacked the settlers during the War of 1812.

Holmes, John (1773–1843): representative from Massachusetts, later becoming Senator of Maine after its admission into the Union. Holmes' famous pamphlet, *Mr. Holmes' Letter to the People of Maine*, answered his constituents' objection to the Missouri Compromise, which arbitrated the simultaneous acceptance of free and slave states.

Humphreys, David (1752–1818): after graduating from Yale at age 17, Humphreys joined the American revolutionary movement, eventually ascending to the rank of lieutenant colonel. With the outbreak of Shays' Rebellion (1787), Humphreys was dispatched to quell the tumult. He was a trusted confidant and friend to George Washington, who appointed him the first US Minister to Portugal, and later to Spain, where he facilitated commercial trade with European nations and negotiated diplomatic relationships.

Kercheval, Samuel (c. 1763–1845): historian and author of *History of the Valley of Virginia* (1833) which chronicled the early social and political history of the state. Kercheval was a longtime neighbor and friend of Jefferson's with whom he exchanged much political correspondence.

King George III (1738–1820): British monarch to whom the Declaration of Independence was addressed. During his sixty-year reign, King George's throne was fraught with internal struggles and troubles abroad. After his government imposed restrictions on the colonial move westward – in an effort to mitigate rising costs of military conflict with Native Americans – the American colonies organized their official independence from the King. The Declaration's laundry list of accusations charged the monarch with tyranny and of plundering the American colonies, an indictment that launched the American War of Independence. The reign of George III was the longest in British history until Queen Victoria.

Madison, James (1751–1836): Jefferson's Secretary of State and life-long friend who succeeded Jefferson as the fourth President of the United States. Madison's influence over the written Constitution and Bill of Rights cannot be understated. He also authored significant portions of the *Federalist Papers* – with John Jay and Alexander Hamilton – contributing vitally to debates that shaped the burgeoning Constitution.

Monroe, James (1758–1831): fifth President of the United States and co-organizer, with Madison and Jefferson, of the Republican Party (later the Democratic-Republicans) – a party standing in opposition to the Hamiltonians (who advocated for strong, centralized federal government). Monroe was well regarded for his diplomatic efficacy. He negotiated the Louisiana Purchase, which more than doubled American territory, and is the namesake of the Monroe Doctrine, an address with longstanding importance to American foreign policy.

Randolph, John (c. 1727–1784): Jefferson's cousin, often referred to as 'the Tory' for his allegiance to King George III in the American War of Independence. He left the colonies for the United Kingdom at the onset of the Revolutionary War where he died in 1784.

Shays, Daniel (c. 1747–1825): captain in the Continental Army, Shays settled in Pelham, Massachusetts after the war. Formulating charges of aristocratic tyranny and bureaucratic abuse – largely in response to rising taxes to retroactively fund the American Revolution – Shays led a mass of largely agrarian workers to prevent proceedings of the Massachusetts Supreme Court. Now known as Shays' Rebellion, the armed conflict between the popular agitators and the state and federal governments distressed the nation's most prominent leaders, which perpetrated the consolidation of power in the federal government. Shays was convicted of treason but was pardoned by then-Massachusetts Governor John Hancock in 1788.

Short, William (1759–1849): private secretary to Jefferson in Paris, Jefferson often referred to Short as his 'adoptive son'. Upon Jefferson's departure from France, Short remained in Europe as US Minister to the Netherlands, and then to Spain where he negotiated treaties between that nation and the United States.

Sparks, Jared (1789–1866): a prolific historian and Unitarian minister who published multivolume collections containing the writings and biographies of Washington, Madison, and Franklin. Sparks also purchased and edited the *North American Review*, an important literary journal, and later served as president of Harvard University.

Smith, William Stevens (1755–1816): son-in-law of the second president John Adams and brother-in-law of John Quincy Adams. Stevens served as staff member to three generals in the Revolutionary War before traveling to London as Secretary of Legation. He returned to the US in 1788, was appointed US Marshall of New York, and continued a life of politics until his death.

Taylor, John (1753–1824): member of the Virginia House of Delegates and later a member of the US Senate, Taylor was also a well-known writer who authored significant defenses of Jefferson. Taylor wrote widely on controversial constitutional and economic issues, focusing mostly on Southern agriculture, constitutional politics, and the defense of slavery.

Tyler, John (1790–1862): tenth President of the United States, taking office after the sudden death of President William Henry Harrison in 1841. The son of Virginia Governor John Tyler Sr., he was engaged in politics from early in his life as member of Virginia House of Delegates, and later in the US House of Representatives.

CHRONOLOGY

1743 Born April 13, Shadwell, Virginia

1760 Begins studies at College of William and Mary

1762 Studies in law begin with George Wythe

1769 Construction begins at Monticello; elected to Virginia House of Burgesses

1772 Marries Martha Wayles Skelton; birth of first child, Martha

1774 Authors *Summary View of the Rights of British America*

1775 Appointed to Second Continental Congress

1776 Drafts the Declaration of Independence

1779 Elected Governor of Virginia

1781 End of gubernatorial incumbency; British troops invade Virginia

1782 Death of wife, Martha Jefferson

1783 Treaty of Paris, formally ending the American War of Independence; elected to Congress

1784 Diplomatic mission in Paris, negotiating commercial treaties

1785 Appointed US Minister to France

1787 First broad publication of *Notes on the State of Virginia*

1789 Returns to the United States

1790 Assumes office of Secretary of State under President George Washington

1793 Resigns position as Secretary of State

1796 Elected Vice President under John Adams

1801 Inaugurated as Third President of the United States

1803 Louisiana Purchase, more than doubling territory of the United States

1804 Elected to second presidential term

1809 End of presidency; returns to Monticello

1812 War with England

1815 Congress purchases Jefferson's library to rebuild the Library of Congress

1817 Begins developing University of Virginia's architectural plans

1821 Completes memoirs

1823 Advises President Monroe on crafting the Monroe Doctrine

1825 University of Virginia opens

1826 Authors final letter; dies at Monticello on July 4

THE DECLARATION
OF INDEPENDENCE

From Thomas Jefferson, *"Autobiography"*

In Congress, Friday June 7, 1776. The delegates from Virginia moved in obedience to instructions from their constituents that the Congress should declare that these United colonies are & of right ought to be free & independent states, that they are absolved from all allegiance to the British crown, and that all political connection between them & the state of Great Britain is & ought to be, totally dissolved; that measures should be immediately taken for procuring the assistance of foreign powers, and a Confederation be formed to bind the colonies more closely together.

The house being obliged to attend at that time to some other business, the proposition was referred to the next day, when the members were ordered to attend punctually at ten o'clock.

Saturday June 8. They proceeded to take it into consideration and referred it to a committee of the whole, into which they immediately resolved themselves, and passed that day & Monday the 10th in debating on the subject.

It was argued by Wilson, Robert R. Livingston, E. Rutledge, Dickinson and others

That tho' they were friends to the measures themselves, and saw the impossibility that we should ever again be united with Gr. Britain, yet they were against adopting them at this time:

That the conduct we had formerly observed was wise & proper now, of deferring to take any capital step till the voice of the people drove us into it:

That they were our power, & without them our declarations could not be carried into effect;

That the people of the middle colonies (Maryland, Delaware, Pennsylva, the Jerseys & N. York) were not yet ripe for bidding adieu to British connection, but that they were fast ripening & in a short time would join in the general voice of America:

That the resolution entered into by this house on the 15th of May for suppressing the exercise of all powers derived from the crown, had shown, by the ferment into which it had thrown these middle colonies, that they had not yet accommodated their minds to a separation from the mother country:

That some of them had expressly forbidden their delegates to consent to such a declaration, and others had given no instructions, & consequently no powers to give such consent:

That if the delegates of any particular colony had no power to declare such colony independant, certain they were the others could not declare it for them; the colonies being as yet perfectly independant of each other:

That the assembly of Pennsylvania was now sitting above stairs, their convention would sit within a few days, the convention of New York was now sitting, & those of the Jerseys & Delaware counties would meet on the Monday following, & it was probable these bodies would take up the question of Independance & would declare to their delegates the voice of their state:

That if such a declaration should now be agreed to, these delegates must retire & possibly their colonies might secede from the Union:

That such a secession would weaken us more than could be compensated by any foreign alliance:

That in the event of such a division, foreign powers would either refuse to join themselves to our fortunes, or, having us so much in their power as that desperate declaration would place us, they would insist on terms proportionably more hard and prejudicial:

That we had little reason to expect an alliance with those to whom alone as yet we had cast our eyes:

That France & Spain had reason to be jealous of that rising power which would one day certainly strip them of all their American possessions:

That it was more likely they should form a connection with

the British court, who, if they should find themselves unable otherwise to extricate themselves from their difficulties, would agree to
a partition of our territories, restoring Canada to France, & the
Floridas to Spain, to accomplish for themselves a recovery of these
colonies:

That it would not be long before we should receive certain information of the disposition of the French court, from the agent whom
we had sent to Paris for that purpose:

That if this disposition should be favorable, by waiting the event
of the present campaign, which we all hoped would be successful,
we should have reason to expect an alliance on better terms:

That this would in fact work no delay of any effectual aid from
such ally, as, from the advance of the season & distance of our
situation, it was impossible we could receive any assistance during
this campaign:

That it was prudent to fix among ourselves the terms on which
we should form alliance, before we declared we would form one
at all events:

And that if these were agreed on, & our Declaration of Independance ready by the time our Ambassador should be prepared
to sail, it would be as well as to go into that Declaration at this
day.

On the other side it was urged by J. Adams, Lee, Wythe, and others

That no gentleman had argued against the policy or the right of
separation from Britain, nor had supposed it possible we should
ever renew our connection; that they had only opposed its being
now declared:

That the question was not whether, by a declaration of independance, we should make ourselves what we are not; but whether
we should declare a fact which already exists:

That as to the people or parliament of England, we had alwais
been independent of them, their restraints on our trade deriving
efficacy from our acquiescence only, & not from any rights they
possessed of imposing them, & that so far our connection had
been federal only & was now dissolved by the commencement
of hostilities:

That as to the King, we had been bound to him by allegiance, but that this bond was now dissolved by his assent to the late act of parliament, by which he declares us out of his protection, and by his levying war on us, a fact which had long ago proved us out of his protection; it being a certain position in law that allegiance & protection are reciprocal, the one ceasing when the other is withdrawn:

That James the IId. never declared the people of England out of his protection yet his actions proved it & the parliament declared it:

No delegates then can be denied, or ever want, a power of declaring an existing truth:

That the delegates from the Delaware counties having declared their constituents ready to join, there are only two colonies Pennsylvania & Maryland whose delegates are absolutely tied up, and that these had by their instructions only reserved a right of confirming or rejecting the measure:

That the instructions from Pennsylvania might be accounted for from the times in which they were drawn, near a twelvemonth ago, since which the face of affairs has totally changed:

That within that time it had become apparent that Britain was determined to accept nothing less than a carte-blanche, and that the King's answer to the Lord Mayor Aldermen & common council of London, which had come to hand four days ago, must have satisfied every one of this point:

That the people wait for us to lead the way:

That *they* are in favour of the measure, tho' the instructions given by some of their *representatives* are not:

That the voice of the representatives is not always consonant with the voice of the people, and that this is remarkably the case in these middle colonies:

That the effect of the resolution of the 15th of May has proved this, which, raising the murmurs of some in the colonies of Pennsylvania & Maryland, called forth the opposing voice of the freer part of the people, & proved them to be the majority, even in these colonies:

That the backwardness of these two colonies might be ascribed partly to the influence of proprietary power & connections, & partly to their having not yet been attacked by the enemy:

That these causes were not likely to be soon removed, as there seemed no probability that the enemy would make either of these the seat of this summer's war:

That it would be vain to wait either weeks or months for perfect unanimity, since it was impossible that all men should ever become of one sentiment on any question:

That the conduct of some colonies from the beginning of this contest, had given reason to suspect it was their settled policy to keep in the rear of the confederacy, that their particular prospect might be better, even in the worst event:

That therefore it was necessary for those colonies who had thrown themselves forward & hazarded all from the beginning, to come forward now also, and put all again to their own hazard:

That the history of the Dutch revolution, of whom three states only confederated at first proved that a secession of some colonies would not be so dangerous as some apprehended:

That a declaration of Independence alone could render it consistent with European delicacy for European powers to treat with us, or even to receive an Ambassador from us:

That till this they would not receive our vessels into their ports, nor acknowledge the adjudications of our courts of admiralty to be legitimate, in cases of capture of British vessels:

That though France & Spain may be jealous of our rising power, they must think it will be much more formidable with the addition of Great Britain; and will therefore see it their interest to prevent a coalition; but should they refuse, we shall be but where we are; whereas without trying we shall never know whether they will aid us or not:

That the present campaign may be unsuccessful, & therefore we had better propose an alliance while our affairs wear a hopeful aspect:

That to await the event of this campaign will certainly work delay, because during this summer France may assist us effectually by cutting off those supplies of provisions from England & Ireland on which the enemy's armies here are to depend; or by setting in motion the great power they have collected in the West Indies, & calling our enemy to the defence of the possessions they have there:

That it would be idle to lose time in settling the terms of alliance, till we had first determined we would enter into alliance:

That it is necessary to lose no time in opening a trade for our people, who will want clothes, and will want money too for the paiment of taxes:

And that the only misfortune is that we did not enter into alliance with France six months sooner, as besides opening their ports for the vent of our last year's produce, they might have marched an army into Germany and prevented the petty princes there from selling their unhappy subjects to subdue us.

It appearing in the course of these debates that the colonies of N. York, New Jersey, Pennsylvania, Delaware, Maryland, and South Carolina were not yet matured for falling from the parent stem, but that they were fast advancing to that state, it was thought most prudent to wait a while for them, and to postpone the final decision to July 1. but that this might occasion as little delay as possible a committee was appointed to prepare a declaration of independence. The committee were J. Adams, Dr. Franklin, Roger Sherman, Robert R. Livingston & myself. Committees were also appointed at the same time to prepare a plan of confederation for the colonies, and to state the terms proper to be proposed for foreign alliance. The committee for drawing the declaration of Independence desired me to do it. It was accordingly done, and being approved by them, I reported it to the house on Friday the 28th of June when it was read and ordered to lie on the table. On Monday, the 1st of July the house resolved itself into a committee of the whole & resumed the consideration of the original motion made by the delegates of Virginia, which being again debated through the day, was carried in the affirmative by the votes of N. Hampshire, Connecticut, Massachusetts, Rhode Island, N. Jersey, Maryland, Virginia, N. Carolina, & Georgia. S. Carolina and Pennsylvania voted against it. Delaware having but two members present, they were divided. The delegates for New York declared they were for it themselves & were assured their constituents were for it, but that their instructions having been drawn near a twelvemonth before, when reconciliation was still the general object, they were enjoined by them to do nothing which should impede that object. They therefore thought themselves not justifiable in voting on either side, and asked leave to withdraw from the question, which was given them. The committee rose & reported their resolution to the house. Mr. Edward Rutledge of S. Carolina then requested the determination might be put off to the next day, as he believed his colleagues, tho' they disapproved of the resolution, would then join in it for the sake of unanimity. The ultimate question whether the house would agree to the resolution of the committee was accordingly postponed to the next day, when it was again moved and S. Carolina concurred in voting for it. In the meantime a third member had come post from the Delaware counties and turned the vote of that colony in favour of the resolution. Members of a different sentiment attending that morning from Pennsylvania also, their vote was changed, so that the whole 12 colonies who were authorized to vote at all, gave their voices for it; and within a few days, the convention of N. York approved of it and thus supplied the void occasioned by the withdrawing of her delegates from the vote.

Congress proceeded the same day to consider the declaration of Independance which had been reported & lain on the table the Friday preceding, and on Monday referred to a commee of the whole. The pusillanimous idea that we had friends in England worth keeping terms with, still haunted the minds of many. For this reason those passages which conveyed censures on the people of England were struck out, lest they should give them offence. The clause too, reprobating the enslaving the inhabitants of Africa, was struck out in complaisance to South Carolina and Georgia, who had never attempted to restrain the importation of slaves, and who on the contrary still wished to continue it. Our northern brethren also I believe felt a little tender under those censures; for tho' their people have very few slaves themselves yet they had been pretty considerable carriers of them to others. The debates having taken up the greater parts of the 2d 3d & 4th days of July were, in the evening of the last, closed the declaration was reported by the commee, agreed to by the house and signed by every member present except Mr. Dickinson. As the sentiments of men are known not only by what they receive, but what they reject also, I will state the form of the declaration as originally reported. The parts struck out by Congress shall be distinguished by a black line drawn under them; & those inserted by them shall be placed in the margin or in a concurrent column.[1]

---

[1] In this edition designated by brackets.

A DECLARATION BY THE REPRESENTATIVES OF THE UNITED STATES OF AMERICA, IN GENERAL CONGRESS ASSEMBLED [JEFFERSON'S DRAFT][1]

When in the course of human events it becomes necessary for one people to dissolve the political bands which have connected them with another, and to assume among the powers of the earth the separate & equal station to which the laws of nature and of nature's God entitle them, a decent respect to the opinions of mankind requires that they should declare the causes which impel them to the separation.

We hold these truths to be self-evident: that all men are created equal; that they are endowed by their creator with <u>inherent and</u> [certain] inalienable rights; that among these are life, liberty, & the pursuit of happiness: that to secure these rights, governments are instituted among men, deriving their just powers from the consent of the governed; that whenever any form of government becomes destructive of these ends, it is the right of the people to alter or abolish it, & to institute new government, laying it's foundation on such principles, & organizing it's powers in such form, as to them shall seem most likely to effect their safety & happiness. Prudence indeed will dictate that governments long established should not be changed for light & transient causes; and accordingly all experience hath shown that mankind are more disposed to suffer while evils are sufferable, than to right themselves by abolishing the forms to which they are accustomed. But when a long train of abuses & usurpations <u>begun at a distinguished period and</u> pursuing invariably the same object, evinces a design to reduce them under absolute despotism, it is their right, it is their duty to throw off such government, & to provide new guards for their future security. Such has been the patient sufferance of these colonies; & such is now the necessity which constrains them to <u>expunge</u> [alter] their former systems of government. The history of the present king of Great Britain is a history of <u>unremitting</u> [repeated] injuries & usurpations, <u>among which appears no solitary fact to contradict the uniform tenor of the rest but all have</u> [all having] in direct object the establishment of an absolute tyranny over these states. To prove this let facts be submitted to a candid world <u>for the truth of which we pledge a faith yet unsullied by falsehood.</u>

He has refused his assent to laws the most wholesome & necessary for the public good.

He has forbidden his governors to pass laws of immediate & pressing importance, unless suspended in their operation till his assent should be obtained; & when so suspended, he has utterly neglected to attend to them.

He has refused to pass other laws for the accommodation of large districts of people, unless those people would relinquish the right of representation in the legislature, a right inestimable to them, & formidable to tyrants only.

He has called together legislative bodies at places unusual, uncomfortable, and distant from the depository of their public records, for the sole purpose of fatiguing them into compliance with his measures.

He has dissolved representative houses repeatedly <u>& continually</u> for opposing with manly firmness his invasions on the rights of the people.

He has refused for a long time after such dissolutions to cause others to be elected, whereby the legislative powers, incapable of annihilation, have returned to the people at large for their exercise, the state remaining in the meantime exposed to all the dangers of invasion from without & convulsions within.

He has endeavored to prevent the population of these states; for that purpose obstructing the laws for naturalization of foreigners, refusing to pass others to encourage their migrations hither, & raising the conditions of new appropriations of lands.

He has <u>suffered</u> [obstructed] the administration of justice <u>totally to cease in some of these states</u> [by] refusing his [assent to laws for establishing judiciary powers.]

He has made <u>our</u> judges dependant on his will alone, for the tenure of their offices, & the amount & paiment of their salaries.

He has erected a multitude of new offices <u>by a self assumed power</u> and sent hither swarms of new officers to harass our people and eat out their substance.

He has kept among us in times of peace standing armies <u>and ships of war</u> without the consent of our legislatures.

He has affected to render the military independant of, & superior to the civil power.

He has combined with others to subject us to a jurisdiction foreign to our constitutions & unacknowledged by our laws, giving his assent to their acts of pretended legislation for quartering large bodies of armed troops among us; for protecting them by a mock-trial from punishment for any murders which they should commit on the inhabitants of these states; for cutting off our trade with all parts of the world; for imposing taxes on us without our consent; for depriving us [in many cases] of the benefits of trial by jury; for transporting us beyond seas to be tried for pretended offences; for abolishing the free system of English laws in a neighboring province, establishing therein an arbitrary government, and enlarging it's boundaries, so as to render it at once an example and fit instrument for introducing the same absolute rule into these <u>states</u> [colonies]; for taking away our charters, abolishing our most valuable laws, and altering fundamentally the forms of our governments; for suspending our own legislatures, & declaring themselves invested with power to legislate for us in all cases whatsoever.

He has abdicated government here <u>withdrawing his governors, and declaring us out of his allegiance & protection</u>. [by declaring us out of his protection, and waging war against us.]

He has plundered our seas, ravaged our coasts, burnt our towns, & destroyed the lives of our people.

He is at this time transporting large armies of foreign mercenaries to compleat the works of death, desolation & tyranny already begun with circumstances of cruelty and perfidy [scarcely paralleled in the most barbarous ages, & totally] unworthy the head of a civilized nation.

He has constrained our fellow citizens taken captive on the high seas to bear arms against their country, to become the executioners of their friends & brethren, or to fall themselves by their hands.

He has [excited domestic insurrection among us, & has] endeavored to bring on the inhabitants of our frontiers the merciless Indian savages, whose known rule of warfare is an undistinguished destruction of all ages, sexes, & conditions of existence.

He has incited treasonable insurrections of our fellow-citizens, with the allurements of forfeiture & confiscation of our property.

He has waged cruel war against human nature itself, violating it's most sacred rights of life and liberty in the persons of a distant people who never offended him, captivating & carrying them into slavery in another hemisphere, or to incur miserable death in their transportation thither. This piratical warfare, the opprobium of INFIDEL powers, is the warfare of the CHRISTIAN king of Great Britain. Determined to keep open a market where MEN should be bought & sold, he has prostituted his negative for suppressing every legislative attempt to prohibit or to restrain this execrable commerce. And that this assemblage of horrors might want no fact of distinguished die, he is now exciting those very people to rise in arms among us, and to purchase that liberty of which he has deprived them, by murdering the people on whom he also obtruded them: thus paying off former crimes committed against the LIBERTIES of one people, with crimes which he urges them to commit against the LIVES of another.

In every stage of these oppressions we have petitioned for redress in the most humble terms: our repeated petitions have been answered only by repeated injuries.

A prince whose character is thus marked by every act which may define a tyrant is unfit to be the ruler of a [free] people who mean to be free. Future ages will scarcely believe that the hardiness of one man adventured, within the short compass of twelve years only, to lay a foundation so broad & so undisguised for tyranny over a people fostered & fixed in principles of freedom.

Nor have we been wanting in attentions to our British brethren. We have warned them from time to time of attempts by their legislature to extend a [an unwarrantable] jurisdiction over these our states [us]. We have reminded them of the circumstances of our emigration & settlement here, no one of which could warrant so strange a pretension: that these were effected at the expense of our own blood & treasure, unassisted by the wealth or the strength of Great Britain: that in constituting indeed our several forms of government, we had adopted one common king, thereby laying a foundation for perpetual league

& amity with them: but that submission to their parliament was no part of our constitution, nor ever in idea, if history may be credited: and, we [have] appealed to their native justice and magnanimity as well as to [and we have conjured them by] the ties of our common kindred to disavow these usurpations which were likely to [would inevitably] interrupt our connection and correspondence. They too have been deaf to the voice of justice & of consanguinity, and when occasions have been given them, by the regular course of their laws, of removing from their councils the disturbers of our harmony, they have, by their free election, re-established them in power. At this very time too they are permitting their chief magistrate to send over not only soldiers of our common blood, but Scotch & foreign merce-naries to invade & destroy us. These facts have given the last stab to agonizing affection, and manly spirit bids us to renounce forever these unfeeling brethren. We must [We must therefore] endeavor to forget our former love for them, and hold them as we hold the rest of mankind, enemies in war, in peace friends. We might have been a free and a great people together; but a communication of grandeur & of freedom it seems is below their dignity. Be it so, since they will have it. The road to happiness & to glory is open to us too. We will tread it apart from them, and acquiesce in the necessity which denounces our eternal separation [and hold them as we hold the rest of mankind, enemies in war, in peace friends.]!

We therefore the representatives of the United States of America in General Congress assembled do in the name & by authority of the good people of these states reject & renounce all allegiance & subjection to the kings of Great Britain & all others who may hereafter claim by, through or under them: we utterly dissolve all political connection which may heretofore have subsisted between us & the people or parliament of Great Britain: & finally we do assert & declare these colonies to be free & independent states, & that as free & independent states, they have full power to levy war, conclude peace, contract alliances, establish commerce, & to do all other acts & things which independent states may of right do; that they are absolved from all allegiance to the British crown, and that all political connection between them & the state of Great Britain is, & ought to be, totally dissolved; & that as free & independent states they have full power to levy war, conclude peace, contract alliances, establish commerce & to do all other acts & things which independent states may of right do.

And for the support of this declaration, with a firm reliance on the protection of divine providence we mutually pledge to each other our lives, our fortunes, & our sacred honor.

[We therefore the representatives of the United States of America in General Congress assembled, appealing to the supreme judge of the world for the rectitude of our intentions, do in the name, & by the authority of the good people of these colonies, solemnly publish & declare that these united colonies are & of right ought to be free & independent states; that they are absolved from all allegiance to the British crown, and that all political connection between them & the state of Great Britain is, & ought to be, totally dissolved; & that as free & independent states they have full power to levy war, conclude peace, contract alliances, establish commerce & to do all other acts & things which independent states may of right do.

And for the support of this declaration, with a firm reliance on the protection of divine providence we mutually pledge to each other our lives, our fortunes, & our sacred honor.]

The Declaration thus signed on the 4th, on paper was engrossed on parchment, & signed again on the 2d. of August.

---

[1] Words deleted by Congress are designated by underscoring, and those added by brackets.

THE DECLARATION OF INDEPENDENCE (AS ADOPTED BY CONGRESS)

JULY 4, 1776
The Unanimous Declaration of the Thirteen United States of America

When in the Course of human events it becomes necessary for one people to dissolve the political bands which have connected them with another and to assume among the powers of the earth, the separate and equal station to which the Laws of Nature and of Nature's God entitle them, a decent respect to the opinions of mankind requires that they should declare the causes which impel them to the separation.

We hold these truths to be self-evident, that all men are created equal, that they are endowed by their Creator with certain unalienable Rights, that among these are Life, Liberty and the pursuit of Happiness. – That to secure these rights, Governments are instituted among Men, deriving their just powers from the consent of the governed, – That whenever any Form of Government becomes destructive of these ends, it is the Right of the People to alter or to abolish it, and to institute new Government, laying its foundation on such principles and organizing its powers in such form, as to them shall seem most likely to effect their Safety and Happiness. Prudence, indeed, will dictate that Governments long established should not be changed for light and transient causes; and accordingly all experience hath shewn that mankind are more disposed to suffer, while evils are sufferable than to right themselves by abolishing the forms to which they are accustomed. But when a long train of abuses and usurpations, pursuing invariably the same Object evinces a design to reduce them under absolute Despotism, it is their right, it is their duty, to throw off such Government, and to provide new Guards for their future security. – Such has been the patient sufferance of these Colonies; and such is now the necessity which constrains them to alter their former Systems of Government. The history of the present King of Great Britain is a history of repeated injuries and usurpations, all having in direct object the establishment of an absolute Tyranny over these States. To prove this, let Facts be submitted to a candid world.

He has refused his Assent to Laws, the most wholesome and necessary for the public good.

He has forbidden his Governors to pass Laws of immediate and pressing importance, unless suspended in their operation till his Assent should be obtained; and when so suspended, he has utterly neglected to attend to them.

He has refused to pass other Laws for the accommodation of large districts of people, unless those people would relinquish the right of Representation in the Legislature, a right inestimable to them and formidable to tyrants only.

He has called together legislative bodies at places unusual, uncomfortable, and distant from the depository of their Public Records, for the sole purpose of fatiguing them into compliance with his measures.

He has dissolved Representative Houses repeatedly, for opposing with manly firmness his invasions on the rights of the people.

He has refused for a long time, after such dissolutions, to cause others to be elected, whereby the Legislative Powers, incapable of Annihilation, have returned to the People at large for their exercise; the State remaining in the mean time exposed to all the dangers of invasion from without, and convulsions within.

He has endeavoured to prevent the population of these States; for that purpose obstructing the Laws for Naturalization of Foreigners; refusing to pass others to encourage their migrations hither, and raising the conditions of new Appropriations of Lands.

He has obstructed the Administration of Justice by refusing his Assent to Laws for establishing Judiciary Powers.

He has made Judges dependent on his Will alone for the tenure of their offices, and the amount and payment of their salaries.

He has erected a multitude of New Offices, and sent hither swarms of Officers to harass our people and eat out their substance.

He has kept among us, in times of peace, Standing Armies without the Consent of our legislatures.

He has affected to render the Military independent of and superior to the Civil Power.

He has combined with others to subject us to a jurisdiction foreign to our constitution, and unacknowledged by our laws; giving his Assent to their Acts of pretended Legislation:

For quartering large bodies of armed troops among us:

For protecting them, by a mock Trial from punishment for any Murders which they should commit on the Inhabitants of these States:

For cutting off our Trade with all parts of the world:

For imposing Taxes on us without our Consent:

For depriving us in many cases, of the benefit of Trial by Jury:

For transporting us beyond Seas to be tried for pretended offences:

For abolishing the free System of English Laws in a neighbouring Province, establishing therein an Arbitrary government, and enlarging its Boundaries so as to render it at once an example and fit instrument for introducing the same absolute rule into these Colonies:

For taking away our Charters, abolishing our most valuable Laws and altering fundamentally the Forms of our Governments:

For suspending our own Legislatures, and declaring themselves invested with power to legislate for us in all cases whatsoever.

He has abdicated Government here, by declaring us out of his Protection and waging War against us.

He has plundered our seas, ravaged our coasts, burnt our towns, and destroyed the lives of our people.

He is at this time transporting large Armies of foreign Mercenaries to compleat the works of death, desolation, and tyranny, already begun with circumstances of Cruelty & Perfidy scarcely paralleled in the most barbarous ages, and totally unworthy the Head of a civilized nation.

He has constrained our fellow Citizens taken Captive on the high Seas to bear Arms against their Country, to become the executioners of their friends and Brethren, or to fall themselves by their Hands.

He has excited domestic insurrections amongst us, and has endeavoured to bring on the inhabitants of our frontiers, the merciless Indian Savages whose known rule of warfare, is an undistinguished destruction of all ages, sexes and conditions.

In every stage of these Oppressions We have Petitioned for Redress in the most humble terms: Our repeated Petitions have been answered only by repeated injury. A Prince, whose character is thus marked by every act which may define a Tyrant, is unfit to be the ruler of a free people.

Nor have We been wanting in attentions to our British brethren. We have warned them from time to time of attempts by their legislature to extend an unwarrantable jurisdiction over us. We have reminded them of the circumstances of our emigration and settlement here. We have appealed to their native justice and magnanimity, and we have conjured them by the ties of our common kindred to disavow these usurpations, which would inevitably interrupt our connections and correspondence. They too have been deaf to the voice of justice and of consanguinity. We must, therefore, acquiesce in the necessity, which denounces our Separation, and hold them, as we hold the rest of mankind, Enemies in War, in Peace Friends.

We, therefore, the Representatives of the united States of America, in General Congress, Assembled, appealing to the Supreme Judge of the world for the rectitude of our intentions, do, in the Name, and by Authority of the good People of these Colonies, solemnly publish and declare, That these united Colonies are, and of Right ought to be Free and Independent States, that they are Absolved from all Allegiance to the British Crown, and that all political connection between them and the State of Great Britain, is and ought to be totally dissolved; and that as Free and Independent States, they have full Power to levy War, conclude Peace contract Alliances, establish Commerce, and to do all other Acts and Things which Independent States may of right do. – And for the support of this Declaration, with a firm reliance on the protection of Divine Providence, we mutually pledge to each other our Lives, our Fortunes and our sacred Honor.

REBELLION AGAINST
THE GOVERNMENT

To Edward Carrington
Paris, January. 16, 1787

Dear Sir, – Uncertain whether you might be at New York at the moment of Colo. Franks's arrival, I have inclosed my private letters for Virginia under cover to our delegation in general, which otherwise I would have taken the liberty to inclose particularly to you, as best acquainted with the situation of the persons to whom they are addressed. Should this find you at New York, I will still ask your attention to them. The two large packages addressed to Colo. N. Lewis contain seeds, not valuable enough to pay passage, but which I would wish to be sent by the stage, or any similar quick conveyance. The letters to Colo. Lewis & Mr. Eppes (who take care of my affairs) are particularly interesting to me. The package for Colo. Richd. Cary our judge of Admiralty near Hampton, contains seeds & roots, not to be sent by Post. Whether they had better go by the stage, or by water, you will be the best judge. I beg your pardon for giving you this trouble. But my situation & your goodness will I hope excuse it. In my letter to Mr. Jay, I have mentioned the meeting of the Notables appointed for the 29th inst. It is now put off to the 7th or 8th of next month. This event, which will hardly excite any attention in America, is deemed here the most important one which has taken place in their civil line during the present century. Some promise their country great things from it, some nothing. Our friend de La Fayette was placed on the list originally. Afterwards his name disappeared; but finally was reinstated. This shews that his character here is not considered as an indifferent one; and that it excites agitation. His education in our school has drawn on him a very jealous eye from a court whose principles are the most absolute despotism. But I hope he has nearly passed his crisis. The King, who is a good man, is favorably disposed towards him: & he is supported by powerful family connections, & by the public good will. He is the youngest man of the Notables except one whose office placed him on the list.

The Count de Vergennes has within these ten days had a very severe attack of what is deemed an unfixed gout. He has been well enough however to do business to-day. But anxieties for him are not yet quieted. He is a great & good minister, and an accident to him might endanger the peace of Europe.

The tumults in America, I expected would have produced in Europe an unfavorable opinion of our political state. But it has not. On the contrary, the small effect of these tumults seems to have given more confidence in the firmness of our governments. The interposition of the people themselves on the side of government has had a great effect on the opinion here. I am persuaded myself that the good sense of the people will always be found to be the best army. They may be led astray for a moment, but will soon correct themselves. The people are the only censors of their governors: and even their errors will tend to keep these to the true principles of their institution. To punish these errors too severely would be to suppress the only safeguard of the public liberty. The way to prevent these irregular interpositions of the people is to give them full information of their affairs thro' the channel of the public papers, & to contrive that those papers should penetrate the whole mass of the people. The basis of our governments being the opinion of the people, the very first object should be to keep that right; and were it left to me to decide whether we should have a government without newspapers or newspapers without a government, I should not hesitate a moment to prefer the latter. But I should mean that every man should receive those papers & be capable of reading them. I am convinced that those societies (as the Indians) which live without government enjoy in their general mass an infinitely greater degree of happiness than those who live under the European governments. Among the former, public opinion is in the place of law, & restrains morals as powerfully as laws ever did anywhere. Among the latter, under pretence of governing they have divided their nations into two classes, wolves & sheep. I do not exaggerate. This is a true picture of Europe. Cherish therefore the spirit of our people, and keep alive their attention. Do not be too severe upon their errors, but reclaim them by enlightening them. If once they become inattentive to the public affairs, you & I, & Congress & Assemblies, judges & governors shall all become wolves. It seems to be the law of our general nature, in spite of individual exceptions; and experience declares that man is the only animal which devours his own kind, for I can apply no milder term to the governments of Europe, and to the general prey of the rich on the poor. The want of news has led me into disquisition instead of narration, forgetting you have every day enough of that. I shall be happy to hear from you sometimes, only observing that whatever passes thro' the post is read, & that when you write what should be read by myself only, you must be so good as to confide your letter to some passenger or officer of the packet. I will ask your permission to write to you some-times, and to assure you of the esteem & respect with which I have honour to be Dear Sir your most obedient & most humble servt.

[. . .]

To James Madison
Paris, January 30, 1787

Dear Sir, – My last to you was of the 16th of Dec, since which I have received yours of Nov 25, & Dec 4, which afforded me, as your letters always do, a treat on matters public, individual & oeconomical. I am impatient to learn your sentiments on the late troubles in the Eastern states. So far as I have yet seen, they do not appear to threaten serious consequences. Those states have suffered by the stoppage of the channels of their commerce, which have not yet found other issues. This must render money scarce, and make the people uneasy. This uneasiness has produced acts absolutely unjustifiable; but I hope they will provoke no severities from their governments. A consciousness of those in power that their administration of the public affairs has been honest, may perhaps produce too great a degree of indignation: and those characters wherein fear predominates over hope may apprehend too much from these instances of irregularity. They may conclude too hastily that nature has formed man insusceptible of any other government but that of force, a conclusion not founded in truth, nor experience. Societies exist under three forms sufficiently distinguishable. 1. Without government, as among our Indians. 2. Under governments wherein the will of every one has a just influence, as is the case in England in a slight degree, and in our states, in a great one. 3. Under governments of force: as is the case in all other monarchies and in most of the other republics. To have an idea of the curse of existence under these last, they must be seen. It is a government of wolves over sheep. It is a problem, not clear in my mind, that the 1st condition is not the best. But I believe it to be inconsistent with any great degree of population. The second state has a great deal of good in it. The mass of mankind under that enjoys a precious degree of liberty & happiness. It has its evils too: the principal of which is the turbulence to which it is subject. But weigh this against the oppressions of monarchy, and it becomes nothing. *Malo periculosam libertatem quam quietam servitutem.* Even this evil is productive of good. It prevents the degeneracy of government, and nourishes a general attention to the public affairs. I hold it that a little rebellion now and then is a good thing, & as necessary in the political world as storms in the physical. Unsuccessful rebellions indeed generally establish the encroachments on the rights of the people which have produced them. An observation of this truth should render honest republican governors so mild in their punishment of rebellions, as not to discourage them too much. It is a medicine necessary for the sound health of government. [. . .]

From Abigail Adams
London, January 29, 1787

My Dear Sir – I received by Col. Franks your obliging favour and am very sorry to find your wrist still continues lame; I have known very salutary effects produced by the use of British oil upon a spraind joint. I have sent a servant to see if I can produce some. You may rest assured that if it does no good: it will not do any injury.

With regard to the Tumults in my Native state which you inquire about, I wish I could say that report exagerated them. It is too true Sir that they have been carried to so allarming a Height as to stop the Courts of justice in several Counties. Ignorant, wrestless desperadoes, without conscience or principals, have led a deluded multitude to follow their standard, under pretence of grievances which have no existance but in their immaginations. Some of them were crying out for a paper currency, some for an equal distribution of property, some were for annihilating all debts, other complaning that the Senate was a useless Branch of Government, that the Court of common pleas was unnecessary, and that the sitting of the General Court in Boston was a grievance. By this list you will see the materials which compose this rebellion, and the necessity there is of the wisest and most vigorus measures to quell and suppress it. Instead of that laudible spirit which you approve, which makes a people watchfull over their Liberties and alert in the defence of them, these mobish insurgents are for sapping the foundation, and distroying the whole fabrick at once. – But as these people make only a small part of the state, when compared to the more sensible and judicious, and altho they create a just allarm and give much trouble and uneasiness, I cannot help flattering myself that they will prove sallutary to the state at large, by leading to an investigation of the causes which have produced these commotions. Luxery and extravagance both in furniture and dress had pervaded all orders of our Countrymen and women, and was hastning fast to sap their independance by involving every class of citizens in distress, and accumulating debts upon them which they were unable to discharge. Vanity was becoming a more powerfull principal than patriotism. The lower order of the community were prest for taxes, and tho possest of landed property they were unable to answer the demand, whilst those who possest money were fearfull of lending, least the mad cry of the mob should force the Legislature upon a measure very different from the touch of Midas.

By the papers I send you, you will see the beneficial effects already produced. An act of the Legislature laying duties of 15 per cent upon many articles of British manufacture and totally prohibiting others – a number of Vollunteers Lawyers physicians and Merchants from Boston made up a party of Light horse commanded by Col. Hitchbourn, Leit. Col. Jackson and Higgenson, and went out in persuit of the insurgents and were fortunate enough to take 3 of their principal Leaders, Shattucks Parker and Page. Shattucks defended himself and was wounded in his knee with a broadsword. He is in Jail in Boston and will no doubt be made an example of.

Your request my dear sir with respect to your Daughter shall be punctually attended to, and you may be assured of every attention in my power towards her.

You will be so kind as to present my Love to Miss Jefferson, compliments to the Marquiss and his Lady. I am really conscience smitten that I have never written to that amiable Lady, whose politeness and attention to me deserved my acknowledgment.

The little balance which you stated in a former Letter in my favour, when an opportunity offers I should like to have in Black Lace at about 8 or 9 Livres pr. Ell. Tho late in the Month, I hope it will not be thought out of season to offer my best wishes for the Health, Long Life and prosperity of yourself and your family, or to assure you of the Sincere Esteem and Friendship with which I am Your's etc. etc. [. . .]

To Abigail Adams
Paris, February 22, 1787

Dear Madam, – I am to acknolege the honor of your letter of Jan. 29. and of the papers you were so good as to send me. They were the latest I had seen or have yet seen. They left off too in a critical moment; just at the point where the Malcontents make their submission on condition of pardon, and before the answer of government was known. I hope they pardoned them. The spirit of resistance to government is so valuable on certain occasions, that I wish it to be always kept alive. It will often be exercised when wrong, but better so than not to be exercised at all. I like a little rebellion now and then. It is like a storm in the Atmosphere. It is wonderful that no letter or paper tells us who is president of Congress, tho' there are letters in Paris to the beginning of January. I suppose I shall hear when I come back from my journey, which will be eight months after he will have been chosen. And yet they complain of us for not giving them intelligence. Our Notables assembled to-day, and I hope before the departure of Mr. Cairnes I shall have heard something of their proceedings worth communicating to Mr. Adams. The most remarkeable effect of this convention as yet is the number of puns and bon mots it has generated. I think were they all collected it would make a more voluminous work than the Encyclopedie. This occasion, more than any thing I have seen, convinces me that this nation is incapable of any serious effort but under the word of command. The people at large view every object only as it may furnish puns and bon mots; and I pronounce that a good punster would disarm the whole nation were they ever so seriously disposed to revolt. Indeed, Madam, they are gone. When a measure so capable of doing good as the calling the Notables is treated with so much ridicule, we may conclude the nation desperate, and in charity pray that heaven may send them good kings. – The bridge at the place Louis XV. is begun. The hotel dieu is to be abandoned and new ones to be built. The old houses on the old bridges are in a course of demolition. This is all I know of Paris. We are about to lose the Count d'Aranda, who has desired and obtained his recall. Fernand Nunnez, before destined for London is to come here. The Abbés Arnoux and Chalut are well. The Dutchess Danville somewhat recovered from the loss of her daughter. Mrs. Barrett very homesick, and fancying herself otherwise sick. They will probably remove to Honfleur. This is all our news. I have only to add then that Mr. Cairnes has taken charge of 15. aunes of black lace for you at 9 livres the aune, purchased by Petit and therefore I hope better purchased than some things have been for you; and that I am with sincere esteem Dear Madam your affectionate humble servt. [. . .]

To David Hartley
Paris, July 2, 1787

Dear Sir, – I received lately your favor of April the 23rd, on my return from a journey of three or four months; and am always happy in an occasion of recalling myself to your memory. The most interesting intelligence from America, is that respecting the late insurrection in Massachusetts. The cause of this has not been developed to me to my perfect satisfaction. The most probable is, that those individuals were of the imprudent number of those, who have involved themselves in debt beyond their abilities to pay, and that a vigorous effort in that government to compel the payment of private debts, and raise money for public ones, produced the resistance. I believe you may be assured that an idea or desire of returning to any thing like their antient form of government, never entered into their heads. I am not discouraged by this. For thus I calculate. An insurrection in one of thirteen States, in the course of eleven years, amounts to one in any particular State, in one hundred and forty-three years, say a century and a half. This would not be near as many, as have happened in any other government that has ever existed. So that we shall have the difference between a light and a heavy government, as clear gain. I have no fear, but that the result of our experiment will be, that men can be trusted to govern themselves without a master. Could the contrary of this be proved, I should conclude, either that there is no God, or that he is a malevolent being. You have heard of the federal convention, now sitting at Philadelphia, for the amendment of the Confederation. Eleven States, appointed delegates certainly; it was expected that Connecticut also would appoint, the moment its Assembly met. Rhode Island had refused. I expect they will propose several amendments; that that relative to our commerce, will be adopted immediately, but that the others must wait to be adopted, one after another, in proportion as the minds of the States ripen to them. Dr Franklin enjoys good health. I shall always be happy to hear from you, being with sentiments of very sincere esteem and respect, Dear Sir, your most obedient and most humble servant [. . .]

To William S. Smith
Paris, November 13, 1787

Dear Sir, – I am now to acknoledge the receipt of your favors of October the 4th, 8th, & 26th. In the last you apologise for your letters of introduction to Americans coming here. It is so far from needing apology on your part, that it calls for thanks on mine. I endeavor to shew civilities to all the Americans who come here, & will give me opportunities of doing it: and it is a matter of comfort to know from a good quarter what they are, & how far I may go in my attentions to them. Can you send me Woodmason's bills for the two copying presses for the M. de la Fayette, & the M. de Chastellux? The latter makes one article in a considerable account, of old standing, and which I cannot present for want of this article. – I do not know whether it is to yourself or Mr. Adams I am to give my thanks for the copy of the new constitution. I beg leave through you to place them where due. It will be yet three weeks before I shall receive them from America. There are very good articles in it: & very bad. I do not know which preponderate. What we have lately read in the history of Holland, in the chapter on the Stadtholder, would have sufficed to set me against a chief magistrate eligible for a long duration, if I had ever been disposed towards one: & what we have always read of the elections of Polish kings should have forever excluded the idea of one continuable for life. Wonderful is the effect of impudent & persevering lying. The British ministry have so long hired their gazetteers to repeat and model into every form lies about our being in anarchy, that the world has at length believed them, the English nation has believed them, the ministers themselves have come to believe them, & what is more wonderful, we have believed them ourselves. Yet where does this anarchy exist? Where did it ever exist, except in the single instance of Massachusetts? And can history produce an instance of rebellion so honourably conducted? I say nothing of it's motives. They were founded in ignorance, not wickedness. God forbid we should ever be 20 years without such a rebellion. The people cannot be all, & always, well informed. The part which is wrong will be discontented in proportion to the importance of the facts they misconceive. If they remain quiet under such misconceptions it is a lethargy, the forerunner of death to the public liberty. We have had 13 states independent 11 years. There has been one rebellion. That comes to one rebellion in a century & a half for each state. What country before ever existed a century & half without a rebellion? & what country can preserve it's liberties if their rulers are not warned from time to time that their people preserve the spirit of resistance? Let them take arms. The remedy is to set them right as to facts, pardon & pacify them. What signify a few lives lost in a century or two? The tree of liberty must be refreshed from time to time with the blood of patriots & tyrants. It is it's natural manure. Our Convention has been too much impressed by the insurrection of Massachusetts: and in the spur of the moment they are setting up a kite to keep the hen-yard in order. I hope in God this article will be rectified before the new constitution is accepted. – You ask me if any thing transpires here on the subject of S. America? Not a word. I know that there are combustible materials there, and that they wait the torch only. But this country probably will join the extinguishers. – The want of facts worth communicating to you has occasioned me to give a little loose to dissertation. We must be contented to amuse, when we cannot inform.[. . .]

THE FRENCH REVOLUTION

To James Madison
Fontainebleau, October 28, 1785

Dear Sir, – Seven o'clock, and retired to my fireside, I have determined to enter into conversation with you. This is a village of about 15,000 inhabitants when the court is not here, and 20,000 when they are, occupying a valley through which runs a brook and on each side of it a ridge of small mountains, most of which are naked rock. The King comes here, in the fall always, to hunt. His court attend him, as do also the foreign diplomatic corps; but as this is not indispensably required and my finances do not admit the expense of a continued residence here, I propose to come occasionally to attend the King's levees, returning again to Paris, distant forty miles. This being the first trip, I set out yesterday morning to take a view of the place. For this purpose I shaped my course towards the highest of the mountains in sight, to the top of which was about a league.

As soon as I had got clear of the town I fell in with a poor woman walking at the same rate with myself and going the same course. Wishing to know the condition of the laboring poor I entered into conversation with her, which I began by enquiries for the path which would lead me into the mountain: and thence proceeded to enquiries into her vocation, condition and circumstances. She told me she was a day laborer at 8 sous or 4d. sterling the day: that she had two children to maintain, and to pay a rent of 30 livres for her house (which would consume the hire of 75 days), that often she could find no employment and of course was without bread. As we had walked together near a mile and she had so far served me as a guide, I gave her, on parting, 24 sous. She burst into tears of a gratitude which could perceive was unfeigned because she was unable to utter a word. She had probably never before received so great an aid. This little *attendrissement*, with the solitude of my walk, led me into a train of reflections on that unequal division of property which occasions the numberless instances of wretchedness which I had observed in this country and is to be observed all over Europe.

The property of this country is absolutely concentred in a very few hands, having revenues of from half a million of guineas a year downwards. These employ the flower of the country as servants, some of them having as many as 200 domestics, not laboring. They employ also a great number of manufacturers and tradesmen, and lastly the class of laboring husbandmen. But after all there comes the most numerous of all classes, that is, the poor who cannot find work. I asked myself what could be the reason so many should be permitted to beg who are willing to work, in a country where there is a very considerable proportion of uncultivated lands? These lands are undisturbed only for the sake of game. It should seem then that it must be because of the enormous wealth of the proprietors which places them above attention to the increase of their revenues by permitting these lands to be labored. I am conscious that an equal division of property is impracticable, but the consequences of this enormous inequality producing so much misery to the bulk of mankind, legislators cannot invent too many devices for subdividing property, only taking care to let their subdivisions go hand in hand with the natural affections of the human mind. The descent of property of every kind therefore to all the children, or to all the brothers and sisters, or other relations in equal degree, is a politic measure and a practicable one. Another means of silently lessening the inequality of property is to exempt all from taxation below a certain point, and to tax the higher portions or property in geometrical progression as they rise. Whenever there are in any country uncultivated lands and unemployed poor, it is clear that the laws of property have been so far extended as to violate natural right. The earth is given as a common stock for man to labor and live on. If for the encouragement of industry we allow it to be appropriated, we must take care that other employment be provided to those excluded from the appropriation. If we do not, the fundamental right to labor the earth returns to the unemployed. It is too soon yet in our country to say that every man who cannot find employment,

but who can find uncultivated land, shall be at liberty to cultivate it, paying a moderate rent. But it is not too soon to provide by every possible means that as few as possible shall be without a little portion of land. The small landholders are the most precious part of a state.
[. . .]

To David Humphreys
Paris, March 18, 1789

Dear Sir, – Your favor of Nov. 29, 1788, came to hand the last month. How it happened that mine of Aug. 1787, was fourteen months on it's way is inconceivable. I do not recollect by what conveyance I sent it. I had concluded however either that it had miscarried or that you had become indolent as most of our countrymen are in matters of correspondence.

The change in this country since you left it is such as you can form no idea of. The frivolities of conversation have given way entirely to politics. Men, women & children talk of nothing else: and all you know talk a great deal. The press groans with daily productions, which in point of boldness make an Englishman stare, who hitherto has thought himself the boldest of men. A complete revolution in this government has, within the space of two years (for it began with the Notables of 1787) been effected merely the force of public opinion, aided indeed by the want of money which the dissipations of the court had brought on. And this revolution has not cost a single life, unless we charge to it a little riot lately in Bretagne which began about the price of bread, became afterwards political and ended in the loss of 4 or 5 lives. The assembly of the states general begins the 27th of April. The representation of the people will be perfect. But they will be alloyed by an equal number of nobility & clergy. The first great question they will have to decide will be whether they shall vote by orders or persons, & I have hopes that the majority of the nobles are already disposed to join the *tiers état*, and this is an army more powerful in France than the 200,000 men of the king. Add to this that the court itself is for the *tiers état*, as the only agent which can relieve their wants; not by giving money themselves (they are squeezed to the last drop) but by pressing it from the non-contributing orders. The king stands engaged to pretend no more to the power of laying, continuing or appropriating taxes, to call the States general periodically, to submit *lettres de cachet* to legal restrictions, to consent to the freedom of the press, and that all this shall be fixed by a fundamental constitution which shall bind his successors. He has not offered a participation in the legislature, but it will surely be insisted on. The public mind is so ripened on all these subjects, that there seems to be now but one opinion. The clergy indeed think separately, & the old men among the Nobles. But their voice is suppressed by the general one of the nation. The writings published on this occasion are some of them very valuable: because, unfettered by the prejudices under which the English labour, they give a full scope to reason, and strike out truths as yet unperceived & unacknoleged on the other side of the channel. An Englishman, dosing under a kind of half reformation, is not excited to think by such gross absurdities as stare a Frenchman in the face wherever he looks, whether it be towards the throne or the altar. *In fine*, I believe this nation will in the course of the present year have as full a portion of liberty dealt out to them as the nation can bear at present, considering how uninformed the mass of their people is [. . .]

[. . .]

I presume that your correspondents here have given you a history of all the events which have happened. The Leyden gazette, tho' it contains several inconsiderable errors, gives on the whole a just enough idea. It is impossible to conceive a greater fermentation than has worked in Paris, nor do I believe that so great a fermentation ever produced so little injury in any other place. I have been thro' it daily, have observed the mobs with my own eyes in order to be satisfied of their objects, and declare to you that I saw so plainly the legitimacy of them, that I have slept in my house as quietly thro' the whole as ever did in the most peaceable moments. So strongly fortified was the despotism of this government by long possession, by the respect & the fears of the people, by possessing the public force, by the imposing authority of forms and of faste, that had it held itself on the defensive only, the national assembly with all their good sense, would probably have only obtained a considerable improvement of the government, not a total revision of it. But, ill informed of the spirit of their nation, the despots around the throne had recourse to violent measures, the forerunners of force. In this they have been completely overthrown, & the nation has made a total resumption of rights, which they had certainly never before ventured even to think of. The National assembly have now as clean a canvas to work on here as we had in America. Such has been the firmness and wisdom of their proceedings in moments of adversity as well as prosperity, that I have the highest confidence that they will use their power justly. As far as

I can collect from conversation with their members, the constitution they will propose will resemble that of England in it's outlines, but not in it's defects. They will certainly leave the king possessed completely of the Executive powers, & particularly of the public force. Their legislature will consist of one order only, & not of two as in England: the representation will be equal & not abominably partial as that of England: it will be guarded against corruption, instead of having a majority sold to the king, & rendering his will absolute: whether it will be in one chamber, or broke into two cannot be foreseen. They will meet at certain epochs & sit as long as they please, instead of meeting only when, & sitting only as long as the king pleases as in England. There is a difference of opinion whether the king shall have an absolute, or only a qualified Negative on their acts. The parliaments will probably be suppressed; & juries provided in criminal cases perhaps even in civil ones. This is what appears probable at present. The Assembly is this day discussing the question whether they will have a declaration of rights. Paris has been led by events to assume the government of itself. It has hitherto worn too much the appearance of conformity to continue thus independently of the will of the nation. Reflection will probably make them sensible that the security of all depends on the dependance of all on the national legislature. I have so much confidence on the good sense of man, and his qualifications for self-government, that I am never afraid of the issue where reason is left free to exert her force; and I will agree to be stoned as a false prophet if all does not end well in this country. Nor will it end with this country. Hers is but the first chapter of the history of European liberty.[. . .]

To William Short
Philadelphia, January 3, 1793

Dear Sir, – My last private letter to you was of Oct. 16. since which I have received your No. 103, 107, 108, 109, 110, 112, 113 & 114 and yesterday your private one of Sep 15, came to hand. The tone of your letters had for some time given me pain, on account of the extreme warmth with which they censured the proceedings of the Jacobins of France. I considered that sect as the same with the Republican patriots, & the Feuillants as the Monarchical patriots, well known in the early part of the revolution, & but little distant in their views, both having in object the establishment of a free constitution, & differing only on the question whether their chief Executive should be hereditary or not. The Jacobins (as since called) yielded to the Feuillants & tried the experiment of retaining their hereditary Executive. The experiment failed completely, and would have brought on the reestablishment of despotism had it been pursued. The Jacobins saw this, and that the expunging that officer was of absolute necessity. And the Nation was with them in opinion, for however they might have been formerly for the constitution framed by the first assembly, they were come over from their hope in it, and were now generally Jacobins. In the struggle which was necessary, many guilty persons fell without the forms of trial, and with them some innocent. These I deplore as much as any body, & shall deplore some of them to the day of my death. But I deplore them as I should have done had they fallen in battle. It was necessary to use the arm of the people, a machine not quite so blind as balls and bombs, but blind to a certain degree. A few of their cordial friends met at their hands the fate of enemies. But time and truth will rescue & embalm their memories, while their posterity will be enjoying that very liberty for which they would never have hesitated to offer up their lives. The liberty of the whole earth was depending on the issue of the contest, and was ever such a prize won with so little innocent blood? My own affections have been deeply wounded by some of the martyrs to this cause, but rather than it should have failed, I would have seen half the earth desolated. Were there but an Adam & an Eve left in every country, & left free, it would be better than as it now is. I have expressed to you my sentiments, because they are really those of 99. in an hundred of our citizens. The universal feasts, and rejoicings which have lately been had on account of the successes of the French shewed the genuine effusions of their hearts. You have been wounded by the sufferings of your friends, and have by this circumstance been hurried into a temper of mind which would be extremely disrelished if known to your countrymen. The *reserve of the President of the United States* had never permitted me to discover the light in which he viewed it, and as I was more anxious that you should satisfy him than me, I had still avoided explanations with you on the subject. But your 113. induced him to break silence and to notice the extreme acrimony of your expressions. He added that he had been informed the sentiments you expressed *in your conversations* were equally offensive to our allies, & that you should consider yourself as the representative of your country and that what you say might be imputed to your constituents. He desired me therefore to write to you on this subject. He added that he considered *France as the sheet anchor of this country and its friendship as a first object*. There are in the U.S. some characters of opposite principles; some of them are high in office, others possessing great wealth, and all of them hostile to France and fondly looking to England as the staff of their hope. These I named to you on a former occasion. Their prospects have certainly not brightened. Excepting them, this country is entirely republican, friends to the constitution, anxious to preserve it and to have it administered according to it's own republican principles. The little party above mentioned have espoused it only as a stepping stone to monarchy, and have endeavored to approximate it to that in it's administration in order to render it's final transition more easy. The successes of republicanism in France have given the coup de grace to their prospects, and I hope to their projects. – I have developed to you faithfully the sentiments of your country, that you may govern yourself accordingly. I know your republicanism to be pure, and that it is no decay of that which has embittered you against it's votaries in France, but too great a sensibility at the partial evil which it's object has been accomplished there. I have written to you in the stile to which I have been always accustomed with you, and which perhaps it is time I should lay aside. But while old men are sensible enough of their own advance in years, they do not sufficiently recollect it in those whom they have seen young. In writing too the last private letter which will probably be written under present circumstances, in contemplating that your correspondence will shortly be turned over to I know not whom, but certainly to some one not in the habit of considering your interests with the same fostering anxieties I do, I have presented things without reserve, satisfied you will ascribe what I have said to it's true motive, use it for your own best interest, and in that fulfil completely what I had in view.

With respect to the subject of your letter of Sep. 15. you will be sensible that many considerations would prevent my undertaking the reformation of a system with which I am so soon to take leave. It is but common decency to leave to my successor the moulding of his own business. – Not knowing how otherwise to convey this letter to you with certainty, I shall appeal to the friendship and honour of the Spanish commissioners here, to give it the protection of their cover, as a letter of private nature altogether. We have no remarkable event here lately, but the death of Dr. Lee; nor have I anything new to communicate to you of your friends or affairs. I am with unalterable affection & wishes for your prosperity, my dear Sir, your sincere friend and servant.[. . .]

To John Breckinridge
Philadelphia, January 29, 1800

Dear Sir, . . . A great revolution has taken place at Paris. The people of that country having never been in the habit of self-government, are not yet in the habit of aknoleging that fundamental law of nature, by which alone self government can be exercised by a society, I mean the *lex majoris partis*. Of the sacredness of this law, our countrymen are impressed from their cradle, so that with them it is almost innate. This single circumstance may possibly decide the fate of the two nations. One party appears to have been prevalent in the Directory & council of 500. the other in the council of antients. Sieyes & Ducos, the minority in the Directory, not being able to carry their points there seem to have gained over Buonaparte, & associating themselves with the majority of the Council of antients, have expelled 120 odd members the most obnoxious of the minority of the Elders, & of the majority of the council of 500. so as to give themselves a majority in the latter council also. 60. were expelled from the 500, so as to change the majority there to the other side. It seems doubtful whether any were expelled from the Antients. The majority there was already with the Consular party. They have established Buonaparte, Sieyes & Ducos into an executive, or rather Dictatorial consulate, given them a committee of between 20. & 30. from each council, & have adjourned to the 20th of Feb. Thus the Constitution of the 3d year which was getting consistency & firmness from time is demolished in an instant, and nothing is said about a new one. How the nation will bear it is yet unknown. Had the Consuls been put to death in the first tumult & before the nation had time to take sides, the Directory & councils might have reestablished themselves on the spot. But that not being done, perhaps it is now to be wished that Buonaparte may be spared, as, according to his protestations, he is for liberty, equality & representative government, and he is more able to keep the nation together, & to ride out the storm than any other. Perhaps it may end in their establishing a single representative & that in his person. I hope it will not be for life, for fear of the influence of the example on our countrymen. It is very material for the latter to be made sensible that their own character & situation are materially different from the French; & that whatever may be the fate of republicanism there, we are able to preserve it inviolate here: we are sensible of the duty & expediency of submitting our opinions to the will of the majority and can wait with patience till they get right if they happen to be at any time wrong. Our vessel is moored at such a distance, that should theirs blow up, ours is still safe, if we will but think so.[. . .]

REPUBLICANISM AND
SELF-GOVERNMENT

To James Madison
Paris, September 6, 1789

Dear Sir, – I sit down to write to you without knowing by what occasion I shall send my letter. I do it because a subject comes into my head which I would wish to develope a little more than is practicable in the hurry of the moment of making up general despatches.

The question Whether one generation of men has a right to bind another, seems never to have been started either on this or our side of the water. Yet it is a question of such consequences as not only to merit decision, but place also, among the fundamental principles of every government. The course of reflection in which we are immersed here on the elementary principles of society has presented this question to my mind; and that no such obligation can be transmitted I think very capable of proof. I set out on this ground which I suppose to be self evident, "*that the earth belongs in usufruct to the living*;" that the dead have neither powers nor rights over it. The portion occupied by an individual ceases to be his when himself ceases to be, and reverts to the society. If the society has formed no rules for the appropriation of its lands in severalty, it will be taken by the first occupants. These will generally be the wife and children of the decedent. If they have formed rules of appropriation, those rules may give it to the wife and children, or to some one of them, or to the legatee of the deceased. So they may give it to his creditor. But the child, the legatee or creditor takes it, not by any natural right, but by a law of the society of which they are members, and to which they are subject. Then no man can by *natural right* oblige the lands he occupied, or the persons who succeed him in that occupation, to the paiment of debts contracted by him. For if he could, he might during his own life, eat up the usufruct of the lands for several generations to come, and then the lands would belong to the dead, and not to the living, which would be reverse of our principle. What is true of every member of the society individually, is true of them all collectively, since the rights of the whole can be no more than the sum of the rights of individuals. To keep our ideas clear when applying them to a multitude, let us suppose a whole generation of men to be born on the same day, to attain mature age on the same day, and to die on the same day, leaving a succeeding generation in the moment of attaining their mature age all together. Let the ripe age be supposed of 21 years, and their period of life 34 years more, that being the average term given by the bills of mortality to persons who have already attained 21 years of age. Each successive generation would, in this way, come on and go off the stage at a fixed moment, as individuals do now. Then I say the earth belongs to each of these generations during it's course, fully, and in their own right. The 2d. generation receives it clear of the debts and incumbrances of the 1st., the 3d. of the 2d. and so on. For if the 1st. could charge it with a debt, then the earth would belong to the dead and not the living generation. Then no generation can contract debts greater than may be paid during the course of it's own existence. At 21 years of age they may bind themselves and their lands for 34 years to come: at 22 for 33: at 23 for 32 and at 54 for one year only; because these are the terms of life which remain to them at those respective epochs. But a material difference must be noted between the succession of an individual and that of a whole generation. Individuals are parts only of a society, subject to the laws of a whole. These laws may appropriate the portion of land occupied by a decedent to his creditor rather than to any other, or to his child, on condition he satisfies his creditor. But when a whole generation, that is, the whole society dies, as in the case we have supposed, and another generation or society succeeds, this forms a whole, and there is no superior who can give their territory to a third society, who may have lent money to their predecessors beyond their faculty of paying.

What is true of a generation all arriving to self-government on the same day, and dying all on the same day, is true of those on a constant course of decay and renewal, with this only difference. A generation coming in and going out entire, as in the first case, would have a right in the 1st year of their self dominion to contract a debt for 33.

years, in the 10th. for 24. in the 20th. for 14. in the 30th. for 4. whereas generations changing daily, by daily deaths and births, have one constant term beginning at the date of their contract, and ending when a majority of those of full age at that date shall be dead. The length of that term may be estimated from the tables of mortality, corrected by the circumstances of climate, occupation &c. peculiar to the country of the contractors. Take, for instance, the table of M. de Buffon wherein he states that 23,994 deaths, and the ages at which they happened. Suppose a society in which 23,994 persons are born every year and live to the ages stated in this table. The conditions of that society will be as follows. 1st. it will consist constantly of 617,703 persons of all ages. 2dly. of those living at any one instant of time, one half will be dead in 24 years 8 months. 3dly. 10,675 will arrive every year at the age of 21 years complete. 4thly. it will constantly have 348,417 persons of all ages above 21 years. 5ly. and the half of those of 21 years and upwards living at any one instant of time will be dead in 18 years 8 months, or say 19 years as the nearest integral number. Then 19 years is the term beyond which neither the representatives of a nation, nor even the whole nation itself assembled, can validly extend a debt.

To render this conclusion palpable by example, suppose that Louis XIV. and XV. had contracted debts in the name of the French nation to the amount of 10.000 milliards of livres and that the whole had been contracted in Genoa. The interest of this sum would be 500 milliards, which is said to be the whole rent-roll, or nett proceeds of the territory of France. Must the present generation of men have retired from the territory in which nature produced them, and ceded it to the Genoese creditors? No. They have the same rights over the soil on which they were produced, as the preceding generations had. They derive these rights not from their predecessors, but from nature. They then and their soil are by nature clear of the debts of their predecessors. Again suppose Louis XV. and his contemporary generation had said to the money lenders of Genoa, give us money that we may eat, drink, and be merry in our day; and on condition you will demand no interest till the end of 19 years, you shall then forever after receive an annual interest of 12.5 per cent. £100 at a compound interest of 6 per cent makes at the end of 19 years an aggregate of principal and interest of £252.14 the interest of which is a £12, 12s, 7d, which is nearly 12 5/8 per cent on the first capital of £100. The money is lent on these conditions, is divided among the living, eaten, drank, and squandered. Would the present generation be obliged to apply the produce of the earth and of their labour to replace their dissipations? Not at all.

I suppose that the received opinion, that the public debts of one generation devolve on the next, has been suggested by our seeing habitually in private life that he who succeeds to lands is required to pay the debts of his ancestor or testator, without considering that this requisition is municipal only, not moral, flowing from the will of the society which has found it convenient to appropriate the lands become vacant by the death of their occupant on the condition of a paiment of his debts; but that between society and society, or generation and generation there is no municipal obligation, no umpire but the law of nature. We seem not to have perceived that, by the law of nature, one generation is to another as one independant nation to another.

The interest of the national debt of France being in fact but a two thousandth part of it's rent-roll, the paiment of it is practicable enough; and so becomes a question merely of honor or expediency. But with respect to future debts; would it not be wise and just for that nation to declare in the constitution they are forming that neither the legislature, nor the nation itself can validly contract more debt, than they may pay within their own age, or within the term of 19 years? And that all future contracts shall be deemed void as to what shall remain unpaid at the end of 19. years from their date? This would put the lenders, and the borrowers also, on their guard. By reducing too the faculty of borrowing within its natural limits, it would bridle the spirit of war, to which too free a course has been procured by the inattention of money lenders to this law of nature, that succeeding generations are not responsible for the preceding.

On similar ground it may be proved that no society can make a perpetual constitution, or even a perpetual law. The earth belongs always to the living generation. They may manage it then, and what proceeds from it, as they please, during their usufruct. They are masters too of their own persons, and consequently may govern them as they please. But persons and property make the sum of the objects of government. The constitution and the laws of their predecessors extinguished them, in their natural course, with those whose will gave them being. This could preserve that being till it ceased to be itself, and no longer. Every constitution, then, and every law, naturally expires at the end of 19 years. If it be enforced longer, it is an act of force and not of right.

It may be said that the succeeding generation exercising in fact the power of repeal, this leaves them as free as if the constitution or law had been expressly limited to 19. years only. In the first place, this objection admits the right, in proposing an equivalent. But the power of repeal is not an equivalent. It might be indeed if every form of government were so perfectly contrived that the will of the majority could always be obtained fairly and without impediment. But this is true of no form. The people cannot assemble themselves; their representation is unequal and vicious. Various checks are opposed to every legislative proposition. Factions get possession of the public councils. Bribery corrupts them. Personal interests lead them astray from the general interests of their constituents; and other impediments arise so as to prove to every practical man that a law of limited duration is much more manageable than one which needs a repeal.

This principle that the earth belongs to the living and not to the dead is of very extensive application and consequences in every country, and most especially in France. It enters into the resolution of the questions Whether the nation may change the descent of lands holden in tail? Whether they may change the appropriation of lands given antiently to the church, to hospitals, colleges, orders of chivalry, and otherwise in perpetuity? whether they may abolish the charges and privileges attached on lands, including the whole catalogue ecclesiastical and feudal? it goes to hereditary offices, authorities and jurisdictions; to hereditary orders, distinctions and appellations; to perpetual monopolies in commerce, the arts or sciences; with a long train of *et ceteras*: and it renders the question of reimbursement a question of generosity and not of right. In all these cases the legislature of the day could authorize such appropriations and establishments for their own time, but no longer; and the present holders, even where they or their ancestors have purchased, are in the case of *bona fide* purchasers of what the seller had no right to convey.

Turn this subject in your mind, my Dear Sir, and particularly as to the power of contracting debts, and develope it with that perspicuity and cogent logic which is so peculiarly yours. Your station in the councils of our country gives you an opportunity of producing it to public consideration, of forcing it into discussion. At first blush it may be rallied as a theoretical speculation; but examination will prove it to be solid and salutary. It would furnish matter for a fine preamble to our first law for appropriating the public revenue; and it will exclude, at the threshold of our new government the contagious and ruinous errors of this quarter of the globe, which have armed despots with means not sanctioned by nature for binding in chains their fellow-men. We have already given, in example one effectual check to the Dog of war, by transferring the power of letting him loose from the executive to the Legislative body, from those who are to spend to those who are to pay. I should be pleased to see this second obstacle held out by us also in the first instance. No nation can make a declaration against the validity of long-contracted debts so disinterestedly as we, since we do not owe a shilling which may not be paid with ease principal and interest, within the time of our own lives. Establish the principle also in the new law to be passed for protecting copy rights and new inventions, by securing the exclusive right for 19 instead of 14 years [a line entirely faded] an instance the more of our taking reason for our guide instead of English precedents, the habit of which fetters us, with all the political herecies of a nation, equally remarkable for it's encitement from some errors, as long slumbering under others. I write you no news, because when an occasion occurs shall write a separate letter for that.[. . .]

To John Tyler
Monticello, May 26, 1810

Dear Sir, – Your friendly letter of the 12th has been duly received. Although I have laid it down as a law to myself, never to embarrass the President with my solicitations, and have not till now broken through it, yet I have made a part of your letter the subject of one to him, and have done it with all my heart, and in the full belief that I serve him and the public in urging that appointment. We have long enough suffered under the base prostitution of law to party passions in one judge, and the imbecility of another. In the hands of one the law is nothing more than an ambiguous text, to be explained by his sophistry into any meaning which may subserve his personal malice. Nor can any milk-and-water associate maintain his own dependance, and by a firm pursuance of what the law really is, extend its protection to the citizens or the public. I believe you will do it, and where you cannot induce your colleague to do what is right, you will be firm enough to hinder him from doing what is wrong, and by opposing sense to sophistry, leave the juries free to follow their own judgment.

I have long lamented with you the depreciation of law science. The opinion seems to be that Blackstone is to us what the Alcoran is to the Mahometans, that everything which is necessary is in him, and what is not in him is not necessary. I still lend my counsel and books to such young students as will fix themselves in the neighborhood. Coke's institutes and reports are their first, and Blackstone their last book, after an intermediate course of two or three years. It is nothing more than an elegant digest of what they will then have acquired from the real fountains of the law. Now men are born scholars, lawyers, doctors; in our day this was confined to poets. You wish to see me again in the legislature, but this is impossible; my mind is now so dissolved in tranquillity, that it can never again encounter a contentious assembly; the habits of thinking and speaking off-hand, after a disuse of five and twenty years, have given place to the slower process of the pen. I have indeed two great measures at heart, without which no republic can maintain itself in strength. 1. That of general education, to enable every man to judge for himself what will secure or endanger his freedom. 2. To divide every county into hundreds, of such size that all the children of each will be within reach of a central school in it. But this division looks to many other fundamental provisions. Every hundred, besides a school, should have a justice of the peace, a constable and a captain of militia. These officers, or some others within the hundred, should be a corporation to manage all its concerns, to take care of its roads, its poor, and its police by patrols, &c., (as the select men of the Eastern townships.) Every hundred should elect one or two jurors to serve where requisite, and all other elections should be made in the hundreds separately, and the votes of all the hundreds be brought together. Our present Captaincies might be declared hundreds for the present, with a power to the courts to alter them occasionally. These little republics would be the main strength of the great one. We owe to them the vigor given to our revolution in its commencement in the Eastern States, and by them the Eastern States were enabled to repeal the embargo in opposition to the Middle, Southern and Western States, and their large and lubberly division into counties which can never be assembled. General orders are given out from a centre to the foreman of every hundred, as to the sergeants of an army, and the whole nation is thrown into energetic action, in the same direction in one instant and as one man, and becomes absolutely irresistible. Could I once see this I should consider it as the dawn of the salvation of the republic, and say with old Simeon, "nunc dimittas Domine." But our children will be as wise as we are, and will establish in the fulness of time those things not yet ripe for establishment. So be it, and to yourself health, happiness and long life.[. . .]

To Joseph C. Cabell
Monticello, February 2, 1816

Dear Sir, [. . .] My letter of the 24th ult. conveyed to you the grounds of the two articles objected to the College bill. Your last presents one of them in a new point of view, that of the commencement of the ward schools as likely to render the law unpopular to the country. It must be a very inconsiderate and rough process of execution that would do this. My idea of the mode of carrying it into execution would be this: Declare the county *ipso facto* divided into wards for the present, by the boundaries of the militia captaincies; somebody attend the ordinary muster of each company, having first desired the captain to call together a full one. There explain the object of the law to the people of the company, put to their vote whether they will have a school established, and the most central and convenient place for it; get them to meet and build a log school-house; have a roll taken of the children who would attend it, and of those of them able to pay. These would probably be sufficient to support a common teacher, instructing gratis the few unable to pay. If there should be a deficiency, it would require too trifling a contribution from the county to be complained of; and especially as the whole county would participate, where necessary, in the same resource. Should the company, by its vote, decide that it would have no school, let them remain without one. The advantages of this proceeding would be that it would become the duty of the alderman elected by the county, to take an active part in pressing the introduction of schools, and to look out for tutors. If, however, it is intended that the State government shall take this business into its own hands, and provide schools for every county, then by all means strike out this provision of our bill. I would never wish that it should be placed on a worse footing than the rest of the State. But if it is believed that these elementary schools will be better managed by the governor and council, the commissioners of the literary fund, or any other general authority of the government, than by the parents within each ward, it is a belief against all experience. Try the principle one step further, and amend the bill so as to commit to the governor and council the management of all our farms, our mills, and merchants' stores. No, my friend, the way to have good and safe government, is not to trust it all to one, but to divide it among the many, distributing to every one exactly the functions he is competent to. Let the national government be entrusted with the defence of the nation, and its foreign and federal relations; the State governments with the civil rights, laws, police, and administration of what concerns the State generally; the counties with the local concerns of the counties, and each ward direct the interests within itself. It is by dividing and subdividing these republics from the great national one down through all its subordinations, until it ends in the administration of every man's farm by himself; by placing under every one what his own eye may superintend, that all will be done for the best. What has destroyed liberty and the rights of man in every government which has ever existed under the sun? The generalizing and concentrating all cares and powers into one body, no matter whether of the autocrats of Russia or France, or of the aristocrats of a Venetian senate. And I do believe that if the Almighty has not decreed that man shall never be free, (and it is a blasphemy to believe it,) that the secret will be found to be in the making himself the depository of the powers respecting himself, so far as he is competent to them, and delegating only what is beyond his competence by a synthetical process, to higher and higher orders of functionaries, so as to trust fewer and fewer powers in proportion as the trustees become more and more oligarchical. The elementary republics of the wards, the county republics, the States republics, and the republic of the Union, would form a gradation of authorities, standing each on the basis of law, holding every one its delegated share of powers, and constituting truly a system of fundamental balances and checks for the government. Where every man is a sharer in the direction of his ward-republic, or of some of the higher ones, and feels that he is a participator in the government of affairs, not merely at an election one day in the year, but every day; when there shall not be a man in the State who will not be a member of some one of its councils, great or small, he will let the heart be torn out of his body sooner than his power be wrested from him by a Caesar or a Bonaparte. How powerfully did we feel the energy of this organization in the case of embargo? I felt the foundations of the government shaken under my feet by the New England townships. There was not an individual in their States whose body was not thrown with all its momentum into action; and although the whole of the other States were known to be in favor of the measure, yet the organization of this little selfish minority enabled it to overrule the Union. What would the unwieldy counties of the middle, the south, and the west do? Call a county meeting, and the drunken loungers at and about the court houses would have collected, the distances being too great for the good people and the industrious generally to attend. The character of those who really met would have been the measure of the weight they would have had in the scale of public opinion. As Cato, then, concluded every speech with the words, *"Carthago delenda est,"* so do I every opinion, with the injunction, "divide the counties into wards." Begin them only for a single purpose; they will soon show for what others they are the best instruments. God bless you, and all our rulers, and give them the wisdom, as I am sure they have the will, to fortify us against the degeneracy of one government, and the concentration of all its powers in the hands of the one, the few, the well-born or the many.[. . .]

To John Taylor
Monticello, May 28, 1816

Dear Sir, – On my return from a long journey and considerable absence from home, I found here the copy of your "Enquiry into the principles of our government," which you had been so kind as to send me; and for which I pray you to accept my thanks. The difficulties of getting new works in our situation, inland and without a single bookstore, are such as had prevented my obtaining a copy before; and letters which had accumulated during my absence, and were calling for answers, have not yet permitted me to give to the whole a thorough reading; yet certain that you and I could not think differently on the fundamentals of rightful government, I was impatient, and availed myself of the intervals of repose from the writing table, to obtain a cursory idea of the body of the work.

I see in it much matter for profound reflection; much which should confirm our adhesion, in practice, to the good principles of our constitution, and fix our attention on what is yet to be made good. The sixth section on the good moral principles of our government, I found so interesting and replete with sound principles, as to postpone my letter-writing to its thorough perusal and consideration. Besides much other good matter, it settles unanswerably the right of instructing representatives, and their duty to obey. The system of banking we have both equally and ever reprobated. I contemplate it as a blot left in all our constitutions, which, if not covered, will end in their destruction, which is already hit by the gamblers in corruption, and is sweeping away in its progress the fortunes and morals of our citizens. Funding I consider as limited, rightfully, to a redemption of the debt within the lives of a majority of the generation contracting it; every generation coming equally, by the laws of the Creator of the world, to the free possession of the earth he made for their subsistence, unincumbered by their predecessors, who, like them, were but tenants for life. You have successfully and completely pulverized Mr. Adams' system of orders, and his opening the mantle of republicanism to every government of laws, whether consistent or not with natural right. Indeed, it must be acknowledged, that the term *republic* is of very vague application in every language. Witness the self-styled republics of Holland, Switzerland, Genoa, Venice, Poland. Were I to assign to this term a precise and definite idea, I would say, purely and simply, it means a government by its citizens in mass, acting directly and personally, according to rules established by the majority; and that every other government is more or less republican, in proportion as it has in its composition more or less of this ingredient of the direct action of the citizens. Such a government is evidently restrained to very narrow limits of space and population. I doubt if it would be practicable beyond the extent of a New England township. The first shade from this pure element, which, like that of pure vital air, cannot sustain life of itself, would be where the powers of the government, being divided, should be exercised each by representatives chosen either *pro hac vice*, or for such short terms as should render secure the duty of expressing the will of their constituents. This I should consider as the nearest approach to a pure republic, which is practicable on a large scale of country or population. And we have examples of it in some of our States constitutions, which, if not poisoned by priest-craft, would prove its excellence over all mixtures with other elements; and, with only equal doses of poison, would still be the best. Other shades of republicanism may be found in other forms of government, where the executive, judiciary and legislative functions, and the different branches of the latter, are chosen by the people more or less directly, for longer terms of years or for life, or made hereditary; or where there are mixtures of authorities, some dependent on, and others independent of the people. The further the departure from direct and constant control by the citizens, the less has the government of the ingredient of republicanism; evidently none where the authorities are hereditary, as in France, Venice, &c., or self-chosen, as in Holland; and little, where for life, in proportion as the life continues in being after the act of election.

The purest republican feature in the government of our own State, is the House of Representatives. The Senate is equally so the first year, less the second, and so on. The Executive still less, because not chosen by the people directly. The Judiciary seriously anti-republican, because for life; and the national arm wielded, as you observe, by military leaders irresponsible but to themselves. Add to this the vicious constitution of our county courts (to whom the justice, the executive administration, the taxation, police, the military appointments of the county, and nearly all our daily concerns are confided), self-appointed, self-continued, holding their authorities for life, and with an impossibility of breaking in on the perpetual succession of any faction once possessed of the bench. They are in truth, the executive, the judiciary, and the military of their respective counties, and the sum of the counties makes the State. And add, also, that one half of our brethren who fight and pay taxes, are excluded, like Helots, from the rights of representation, as if society were instituted for the soil, and not for the men inhabiting it; or one half of these could dispose of the rights and the will of the other half, without their consent.

"What constitutes a State?

Not high-raised battlements, or labor'd mound,

Thick wall, or moated gate;

Not cities proud, with spires and turrets crown'd;

No: men, high minded men;

Men, who their duties know;

But know their rights; and knowing, dare maintain.

These constitute a State."

In the General Government, the House of Representatives is mainly republican; the Senate scarcely so at all, as not elected by the people directly, and so long secured even against those who do elect them; the Executive more republican than the Senate, from its shorter term, its election by the people, in *practice*, (for they vote for A only on an assurance that he will vote for B,) and because, *in practice also*, a principle of rotation seems to be in a course of establishment; the judiciary independent of the nation, their coercion by impeachment being found nugatory.

If, then, the control of the people over the organs of their government be the measure of its republicanism, and confess I know no other measure, it must be agreed that our governments have much less of republicanism than ought to have been expected; in other words, that the people have less regular control over their agents, than their rights and their interests require. And this I ascribe, not to any want of republican dispositions in those who formed these constitutions, but to a submission of true principle to European authorities, to speculators on government, whose fears of the people have been inspired by the populace of their own great cities, and were unjustly entertained against the independent, the happy, and therefore orderly citizens of the United States. Much apprehend that the golden moment is past for reforming these heresies. The functionaries of public power rarely strengthen in their dispositions to abridge it, and an unorganized call for timely amendment is not likely to prevail against an organized opposition to it. We are always told that things are going on well; why change them? *"Chi sta bene, non si muove,"* said the Italian, "let him who stands well, stand still." This is true; and I verily believe they would go on well with us under an absolute monarch, while our present character remains, of order, industry and love of peace, and restrained, as he would be, by the proper spirit of the people. But it is while it remains such, we should provide against the consequences of its deterioration. And let us rest in the hope that it will yet be done, and spare ourselves the pain of evils which may never happen.

On this view of the import of the term *republic*, instead of saying, as has been said, "that it may mean anything or nothing," we may say with truth and meaning, that governments are more or less republican as they have more or less of the element of popular election and control in their composition; and believing, as I do, that the mass of the citizens is the safest depository of their own rights, and especially, that the evils flowing from the duperies of the people, are less injurious than those from the egoism of their agents, I am a friend to that composition of government which has in it the most of this ingredient. And I sincerely believe, with you, that banking establishments are more dangerous than standing armies; and that the principle of spending money to be paid by posterity, under the name of funding, is but swindling futurity on a large scale.

I salute you with constant friendship and respect.[. . .]

To Samuel Kercheval
Monticello, July 12, 1816

Sir, – I duly received your favor of June the 13th, with the copy of the letters on the calling a convention, on which you are pleased to ask my opinion. I have not been in the habit of mysterious reserve on any subject, nor of buttoning up my opinions within my own doublet. On the contrary, while in public service especially, I thought the public entitled to frankness, and intimately to know whom they employed. But I am now retired: I resign myself, as a passenger, with confidence to those at present at the helm, and ask but for rest, peace and good will. The question you propose, on equal representation, has become a party one, in which I wish to take no public share. Yet, if it be asked for your own satisfaction only, and not to be quoted before the public, I have no motive to withhold it, and the less from you, as it coincides with your own. At the birth of our republic, I committed that opinion to the world, in the draught of a constitution annexed to the "Notes on Virginia," in which a provision was inserted for a representation permanently equal. The infancy of the subject at that moment, and our inexperience of self-government, occasioned gross departures in that draught from genuine republican canons. In truth, the abuses of monarchy had so much filled all the space of political contemplation, that we imagined everything republican which was not monarchy. We had not yet penetrated to the mother principle, that "governments are republican only in proportion as they embody the will of their people, and execute it." Hence, our first constitutions had really no leading principles in them. But experience and reflection have but more and more confirmed me in the particular importance of the equal representation then proposed. On that point, then, I am entirely in sentiment with your letters; and only lament that a copyright of your pamphlet prevents their appearance in the newspapers, where alone they would be generally read, and produce general effect. The present vacancy too, of other matter, would give them place in every paper, and bring the question home to every man's conscience.

But inequality of representation in both Houses of our legislature, is not the only republican heresy in this first essay of our revolutionary patriots at forming a constitution. For let it be agreed that a government is republican in proportion as every member composing it has his equal voice in the direction of its concerns (not indeed in person, which would be impracticable beyond the limits of a city, or small township, but) by representatives chosen by himself, and responsible to him at short periods, and let us bring to the test of this canon every branch of our constitution.

In the legislature, the House of Representatives is chosen by less than half the people, and not at all in proportion to those who do choose. The Senate are still more disproportionate, and for long terms of irresponsibility. In the Executive, the Governor is entirely independent of the choice of the people, and of their control; his Council equally so, and at best but a fifth wheel to a wagon. In the Judiciary, the judges of the highest courts are dependent on none but themselves. In England, where judges were named and removable at the will of an hereditary executive, from which branch most misrule was feared, and has flowed, it was a great point gained, by fixing them for life, to make them independent of that executive. But in a government founded on the public will, this principle operates in an opposite direction, and against that will. There, too, they were still removable on a concurrence of the executive and legislative branches. But we have made them independent of the nation itself. They are irremovable, but by their own body, for any depravities of conduct, and even by their own body for the imbecilities of dotage. The justices of the inferior courts are self-chosen, are for life, and perpetuate their own body in succession forever, so that a faction once possessing themselves of the bench of a county, can never be broken up, but hold their county in chains, forever indissoluble. Yet these justices are the real executive as well as judiciary, in all our minor and most ordinary concerns. They tax us at will; fill the office of sheriff, the most important of all the executive officers of the county; name nearly all our military leaders, which leaders, once named, are removable but by themselves. The juries, our judges of all fact, and of law when they choose it, are not selected by the people, nor amenable to them. They are chosen by an officer named by the court and executive. Chosen, did I say? Picked up by the sheriff from the loungings of the court yard, after everything respectable has retired from it. Where then is our republicanism to be found? Not in our constitution certainly, but merely in the spirit of our people. That would oblige even a despot to govern us republicanly. Owing to this spirit, and to nothing in the form of our constitution, all things have gone well. But this fact, so triumphantly misquoted by the enemies of reformation, is not the fruit of our constitution, but has prevailed in spite of it. Our functionaries have done well, because generally honest men. If any were not so, they feared to show it.

But it will be said, it is easier to find faults than to amend them. I do not think their amendment so difficult as is pretended. Only lay down true principles, and adhere to them inflexibly. Do not be frightened into their surrender by the alarms of the timid, or the croakings of wealth against the ascendency of the people. If experience be called for, appeal to that of our fifteen or twenty governments for forty years, and show me where the people have done half the mischief in these forty years, that a single despot would have done in a single year; or show half the riots and rebellions, the crimes and the punishments, which have taken place in any single nation, under kingly government, during the same period. The true foundation of republican government is the equal right of every citizen, in his person and property, and in their management. Try by this, as a tally, every provision of our constitution, and see if it hangs directly on the will of the people. Reduce your legislature to a convenient number for full, but orderly discussion. Let every man who fights or pays, exercise his just and equal right in their election. Submit them to approbation or rejection at short intervals. Let the executive be chosen in the same way, and for the same term, by those whose agent he is to be; and leave no screen of a council behind which to skulk from responsibility. It has been thought that the people are not competent electors of judges *learned in the law*. But I do not know that this is true, and, if doubtful, we should follow principle. In this, as in many other elections, they would be guided by reputation, which would not err oftener, perhaps, than the present mode of appointment. In one State of the Union, at least, it has long been tried, and with the most satisfactory success. The judges of Connecticut have been chosen by the people every six months, for nearly two centuries, and believe there has hardly ever been an instance of change; so powerful is the curb of incessant responsibility. If prejudice, however, derived from a monarchical institution, is still to prevail against the vital elective principle of our own, and if the existing example among ourselves of periodical election of judges by the people be still mistrusted, let us at least not adopt the evil, and reject the good, of the English precedent; let us retain a movability on the concurrence of the executive and legislative branches, and nomination by the executive alone. Nomination to office is an executive function. To give it to the legislature, as we do, is a violation of the principle of the separation of powers. It swerves the members from correctness, by temptations to intrigue for office themselves, and to a corrupt barter of votes; and destroys responsibility by dividing it among a multitude. By leaving nomination in its proper place, among executive functions, the principle of the distribution of power is preserved, and responsibility weighs with its heaviest force on a single head.

The organization of our county administrations may be thought more difficult. But follow principle, and the knot unties itself. Divide the counties into wards of such size as that every citizen can attend, when called on, and act in person. Ascribe to them the government of their wards in all things relating to themselves exclusively. A justice, chosen by themselves, in each, a constable, a military company, a patrol, a school, the care of their own poor, their own portion of the public roads, the choice of one or more jurors to serve in some court, and the delivery, within their own wards, of their own votes for all elective officers of higher sphere, will relieve the county administration of nearly all its business, will have it better done, and by making every citizen an acting member of the government, and in the offices nearest and most interesting to him, will attach him by his strongest feelings to the independence of his country, and its republican constitution. The justices thus chosen by every ward, would constitute the county court, would do its judiciary business, direct roads and bridges, levy county and poor rates, and administer all the matters of common interest to the whole country. These wards, called townships in New England, are the vital principle of their governments, and have proved themselves the wisest invention ever devised by the wit of man for the perfect exercise of self-government, and for its preservation. We should thus marshal our government into, 1, the general federal republic, for all concerns foreign and federal; 2, that of the State, for what relates to our own citizens exclusively; 3, the county republics, for the duties and concerns of the county; and 4, the ward republics, for the small, and yet numerous and interesting concerns of the neighborhood; and in government, as well as in every other business of life, it is by division and subdivision of duties alone, that all matters, great and small, can be managed to perfection. And the whole is cemented by giving to every citizen, personally, a part in the administration of the public affairs.

The sum of these amendments is, 1. General Suffrage. 2. Equal representation in the legislature. 3. An executive chosen by the people. 4. Judges elective or amovable. 5. Justices, jurors, and sheriffs elective. 6. Ward divisions. And 7. Periodical amendments of the constitution.

I have thrown out these as loose heads of amendment, for consideration and correction; and their object is to secure self-government by the republicanism of our constitution, as well as by the spirit of the people; and to nourish and perpetuate that spirit. I am not among those who fear the people. They, and not the rich, are our dependence for continued freedom. And to preserve their independence, we must not let our rulers load us with perpetual debt. We must make our election between *economy and liberty*, or *profusion and servitude*. If we run into such debts, as that we must be taxed in our meat and in our drink, in our necessaries and our comforts, in our labors and our amusements, for our callings and our creeds, as the people of England are, our people, like them, must come to labor sixteen hours in the twenty-four, give the earnings of fifteen of these to the government for their debts and daily expenses; and the sixteenth being insufficient to afford us bread, we must live, as they now do, on oatmeal and potatoes; have no time to think, no means of calling the mismanagers to account; but be glad to obtain subsistence by hiring ourselves to rivet their chains on the necks of our fellow-sufferers. Our landholders, too, like theirs, retaining indeed the title and stewardship of estates called theirs, but held really in trust for the treasury, must wander, like theirs, in foreign countries, and be contented with penury, obscurity, exile, and the glory of the nation. This example reads to us the salutary lesson, that private fortunes are destroyed by public as well as by private extravagance. And this is the tendency of all human governments. A departure from principle in one instance becomes a precedent for a second; that second for a third; and so on, till the bulk of the society is reduced to be mere automatons of misery, and to have no sensibilities left but for sinning and suffering. Then begins, indeed, the *bellum omnium in omnia*, which some philosophers observing to be so general in this world, have mistaken it for the natural, instead of the abusive state of man. And the fore horse of this frightful team is public debt. Taxation follows that, and in its train wretchedness and oppression.

Some men look at constitutions with sanctimonious reverence, and deem them like the arc of the covenant, too sacred to be touched. They ascribe to the men of the preceding age a wisdom more than human, and suppose what they did to be beyond amendment. I knew that age well; I belonged to it, and labored with it. It deserved well of its country. It was very like the present, but without the experience of the present; and forty years of experience in government is worth a century of book-reading; and this they would say themselves, were they to rise from the dead. I am certainly not an advocate for frequent and untried changes in laws and constitutions. I think moderate imperfections had better be borne with; because, when once known, we accommodate ourselves to them, and find practical means of correcting their ill effects. But I know also, that laws and institutions must go hand in hand with the progress of the human mind. As that becomes more developed, more enlightened, as new discoveries are made, new truths disclosed, and manners and opinions change with the change of circumstances, institutions must advance also, and keep pace with the times. We might as well require a man to wear still the coat which fitted him when a boy, as civilized society to remain ever under the regimen of their barbarous ancestors. It is this preposterous idea which has lately deluged Europe in blood. Their monarchs, instead of wisely yielding to the gradual change of circumstances, of favoring progressive accommodation to progressive improvement, have clung to old abuses, entrenched themselves behind steady habits, and obliged their subjects to seek through blood and violence rash and ruinous innovations, which, had they been referred to the peaceful deliberations and collected wisdom of the nation, would have been put into acceptable and salutary forms. Let us follow no such examples, nor weakly believe that one generation is not as capable as another of taking care of itself, and of ordering its own affairs. Let us, as our sister States have done, avail ourselves of our reason and experience, to correct the crude essays of our first and unexperienced, although wise, virtuous, and well-meaning councils. And lastly, let us provide in our constitution for its revision at stated periods. What these periods should be, nature herself indicates. By the European tables of mortality, of the adults living at any one moment of time, a majority will be dead in about nineteen years. At the end of that period, then, a new majority is come into place; or, in other words, a new generation. Each generation is as independent as the one preceding, as that was of all which had gone before. It has then, like them, a right to choose for itself the form of government it believes most promotive of its own happiness; consequently, to accommodate to the circumstances in which it finds itself, that received from its predecessors; and it is for the peace and good of mankind, that a solemn opportunity of doing this every nineteen or twenty years, should be provided by the constitution; so that it may be handed on, with periodical repairs, from generation to generation, to the end of time, if anything human can so long endure. It is now forty years since the constitution of Virginia was formed. The same tables inform us, that, within that period, two-thirds of the adults then living are now dead. Have then the remaining third, even if they had the wish, the right to hold in obedience to their will, and to laws heretofore made by them, the other two-thirds, who, with themselves, compose the present mass of adults? If they have not, who has? The dead? But the dead have no rights. They are nothing; and nothing cannot own something. Where there is no substance, there can be no accident. This corporeal globe, and everything upon it, belong to its present corporeal inhabitants, during their generation. They alone have a right to direct what is the concern of themselves alone, and to declare the law of that direction; and this declaration can only be made by their majority. That majority, then, has a right to depute representatives to a convention, and to make the constitution what they think will be the best for themselves. But how collect their voice? This is the real difficulty. If invited by private authority, or county or district meetings, these divisions are so large that few will attend; and their voice will be imperfectly, or falsely pronounced. Here, then, would be one of the advantages of the ward divisions I have proposed. The mayor of every ward, on a question like the present, would call his ward together, take the simple yea or nay of its members, convey these to the county court, who would hand on those of all its wards to the proper general authority; and the voice of the whole people would be thus fairly, fully, and peaceably expressed, discussed, and decided by the common reason of the society. If this avenue be shut to the call of sufferance, it will make itself heard through that of force, and we shall go on, as other nations are doing, in the endless circle of oppression, rebellion, reformation; and oppression, rebellion, reformation, again; and so on forever.

These, Sir, are my opinions of the governments we see among men, and of the principles by which alone we may prevent our own from falling into the same dreadful track. I have given them at greater length than your letter called for. But I cannot say things by halves; and I confide them to your honor, so to use them as to preserve me from the gridiron of the public papers. If you shall approve and enforce them, as you have done that of equal representation, they may do some good. If not, keep them to yourself as the effusions of withered age and useless time. I shall, with not the less truth, assure you of my great respect and consideration.[. . .]

NATIVE AMERICANS
AND BLACK SLAVERY

From *Notes on the State of Virginia*

It will probably be asked, Why not retain and incorporate the blacks into the state, and thus save the expence of supplying, by importation of white settlers, the vacancies they will leave? Deep rooted prejudices entertained by the whites; ten thousand recollections, by the blacks, of the injuries they have sustained; new provocations; the real distinctions which nature has made; and many other circumstances, will divide us into parties, and produce convulsions which will probably never end but in the extermination of the one or the other race. – To these objections, which are political, may be added others, which are physical and moral. The first difference which strikes us is that of colour. Whether the black of the negro resides in the reticular membrane between the skin and scarf-skin, or in the scarf-skin itself; whether it proceeds from the colour of the blood, the colour of the bile, or from that of some other secretion, the difference is fixed in nature, and is as real as if its seat and cause were better known to us. And is this difference of no importance? Is it not the foundation of a greater or less share of beauty in the two races? Are not the fine mixtures of red and white, the expressions of every passion by greater or less suffusions of colour in the one, preferable to that eternal monotony, which reigns in the countenances, that immoveable veil of black which covers all the emotions of the other race? Add to these, flowing hair, a more elegant symmetry of form, their own judgment in favour of the whites, declared by their preference of them, as uniformly as is the preference of the Oranootan for the black women over those of his own species. The circumstance of superior beauty, is thought worthy attention in the propagation of our horses, dogs, and other domestic animals; why not in that of man? Besides those of colour, figure, and hair, there are other physical distinctions proving a difference of race. They have less hair on the face and body. They secrete less by the kidnies, and more by the glands of the skin, which gives them a very strong and disagreeable odour. This greater degree of transpiration renders them more tolerant of heat, and less so of cold, than the whites. Perhaps too a difference of structure in the pulmonary apparatus, which a late ingenious experimentalist has discovered to be the principal regulator of animal heat, may have disabled them from extricating, in the act of inspiration, so much of that fluid from the outer air, or obliged them in expiration, to part with more of it. They seem to require less sleep. A black, after hard labour through the day, will be induced by the slightest amusements to sit up till midnight, or later, though knowing he must be out with the first dawn of the morning. They are at least as brave, and more adventuresome. But this may perhaps proceed from a want of fore-thought, which prevents their seeing a danger till it be present. When present, they do not go through it with more coolness or steadiness than the whites. They are more ardent after their female: but love seems with them to be more an eager desire, than a tender delicate mixture of sentiment and sensation. Their griefs are transient. Those numberless afflictions, which render it doubtful whether heaven has given life to us in mercy or in wrath, are less felt, and sooner forgotten with them. In general, their existence appears to participate more of sensation than reflection. To this must be ascribed their disposition to sleep when abstracted from their diversions, and unemployed in labour. An animal whose body is at rest, and who does not reflect, must be disposed to sleep of course. Comparing them by their faculties of memory, reason, and imagination, it appears to me, that in memory they are equal to the whites; in reason much inferior, as I think one could scarcely be found capable of tracing and comprehending the investigations of Euclid; and that in imagination they are dull, tasteless, and anomalous. It would be unfair to follow them to Africa for this investigation. We will consider them here, on the same stage with the whites, and where the facts are not apocryphal on which a judgment is to be formed. It will be right to make great allowances for the difference of condition, of education, of conversation, of the sphere in which they move. Many millions of them have been brought to, and born in America. Most of them indeed have been confined to tillage, to their own homes, and their own society: yet many have been so situated, that they might have availed themselves of the conversation of their masters; many have been brought up to the handicraft arts, and from that circumstance have always been associated with the whites. Some have been liberally educated, and all have lived in countries where the arts and sciences are cultivated to a considerable degree, and have had before their eyes samples of the best works from abroad. The Indians, with no advantages of this kind, will often carve figures on their pipes not destitute of design and merit. They will crayon out an animal, a plant, or a country, so as to prove the existence of a germ in their minds which only wants cultivation. They astonish you with strokes of the most sublime oratory; such as prove their reason and sentiment strong, their imagination glowing and elevated. But never yet could I find that a black had uttered a thought above the level of plain narration; never see even an elementary trait of painting or sculpture. In music they are more generally gifted than the whites with accurate ears for tune and time, and they have been found capable of imagining a small catch. Whether they will be equal to the composition of a more extensive run of melody, or of complicated harmony, is yet to be proved. Misery is often the parent of the most affecting touches in poetry. – Among the blacks is misery enough, God knows, but no poetry. Love is the peculiar oestrum of the poet. Their love is ardent, but it kindles the senses only, not the imagination. Religion indeed has produced a Phyllis Whately; but it could not produce a poet. The compositions published under her name are below the dignity of criticism. The heroes of the Dunciad are to her, as Hercules to the author of that poem. Ignatius Sancho has approached nearer to merit in composition; yet his letters do more honour to the heart than the head. They breathe the purest effusions of friendship and general philanthropy, and shew how great a degree of the latter may be compounded with strong religious zeal. He is often happy in the turn of his compliments, and his stile is easy and familiar, except when he affects a Shandean fabrication of words. But his imagination is wild and extravagant, escapes incessantly from every restraint of reason and taste, and, in the course of its vagaries, leaves a tract of thought as incoherent and eccentric, as is the course of a meteor through the sky. His subjects should often have led him to a process of sober reasoning: yet we find him always substituting sentiment for demonstration. Upon the whole, though we admit him to the first place among those of his own colour who have presented themselves to the public judgment, yet when we compare him with the writers of the race among whom he lived, and particularly with the epistolary class, in which he has taken his own stand, we are compelled to enroll him at the bottom of the column. This criticism supposes the letters published under his name to be genuine, and to have received amendment from no other hand; points which would not be of easy investigation. The improvement of the blacks in body and mind, in the first instance of their mixture with the whites, has been observed by every one, and proves that their inferiority is not the effect merely of their condition of life.

[. . .]

To our reproach it must be said, that though for a century and a half we have had under our eyes the races of black and of red men, they have never yet been viewed by us as subjects of natural history. advance it therefore as a suspicion only, that the blacks, whether originally a distinct race, or made distinct by time and circumstances, are inferior to the whites in the endowments both of body and mind. It is not against experience to suppose, that different species of the same genus, or varieties of the same species, may possess different qualifications. Will not a lover of natural history then, one who views the gradations in all the races of animals with the eye of philosophy, excuse an effort to keep those in the department of man as distinct as nature has formed them? This unfortunate difference of colour, and perhaps of faculty, is a powerful obstacle to the emancipation of these people. Many of their advocates, while they wish to vindicate the liberty of human nature, are anxious also to preserve its dignity and beauty. Some of these, embarrassed by the question "What further is to be done with them?" join themselves in opposition with those who are actuated by sordid avarice only. Among the Romans emancipation required but one effort. The slave, when made free, might mix with, without staining the blood of his master. But with us a second is necessary, unknown to history. When freed, he is to be removed beyond the reach of mixture.[. . .]

From Benjamin Banneker
August 19, 1791

Sir, – I am fully sensible of the greatness of that freedom, which I take with you on the present occasion; a liberty which seemed to me scarcely allowable, when I reflected on that distinguished and dignified station in which you stand, and the almost general prejudice and prepossession, which is so prevalent in the world against those of my complexion.

I suppose it is a truth too well attested to you, to need a proof here, that we are a race of beings, who have long labored under the abuse and censure of the world; that we have long been looked upon with an eye of contempt; and that we have long been considered rather as brutish than human, and scarcely capable of mental endowments.

Sir, I hope I may safely admit, in consequence of that report which hath reached me, that you are a man far less inflexible in sentiments of this nature, than many others; that you are measurably friendly, and well disposed towards us; and that you are willing and ready to lend your aid and assistance to our relief, from those many distresses, and numerous calamities, to which we are reduced. Now Sir, if this is founded in truth, I apprehend you will embrace every opportunity, to eradicate that train of absurd and false ideas and opinions, which so generally prevails with respect to us; and that your sentiments are concurrent with mine, which are, that one universal Father hath given being to us all; and that he hath not only made us all of one flesh, but that he hath also, without partiality, afforded us all the same sensations and endowed us all with the same faculties; and that however variable we may be in society or religion, however diversified in situation or color, we are all of the same family, and stand in the same relation to him.

Sir, if these are sentiments of which you are fully persuaded, I hope you cannot but acknowledge, that it is the indispensable duty of those, who maintain for themselves the rights of human nature, and who possess the obligations of Christianity, to extend their power and influence to the relief of every part of the human race, from whatever burden or oppression they may unjustly labor under; and this, I apprehend, a full conviction of the truth and obligation of these principles should lead all to. Sir, I have long been convinced, that if your love for yourselves, and for those inestimable laws, which preserved to you the rights of human nature, was founded on sincerity, you could not but be solicitous, that every individual, of whatever rank or distinction, might with you equally enjoy the blessings thereof; neither could you rest satisfied short of the most active effusion of your exertions, in order to their promotion from any state of degradation, to which the unjustifiable cruelty and barbarism of men may have reduced them.

Sir, I freely and cheerfully acknowledge, that I am of the African race, and in that color which is natural to them of the deepest dye; and it is under a sense of the most profound gratitude to the Supreme Ruler of the Universe, that I now confess to you, that I am not under that state of tyrannical thraldom, and inhuman captivity, to which too many of my brethren are doomed, but that I have abundantly tasted of the fruition of those blessings, which proceed from that free and unequalled liberty with which you are favored; and which, I hope, you will willingly allow you have mercifully received, from the immediate hand of that Being, from whom proceedeth every good and perfect Gift.

Sir, suffer me to recal to your mind that time, in which the arms and tyranny of the British crown were exerted, with every powerful effort, in order to reduce you to a state of servitude: look back, I entreat you, on the variety of dangers to which you were exposed; reflect on that time, in which every human aid appeared unavailable, and in which even hope and fortitude wore the aspect of inability to the conflict, and you cannot but be led to a serious and grateful sense of your miraculous and providential preservation; you cannot but acknowledge, that the present freedom and tranquility which you enjoy you have mercifully received, and that it is the peculiar blessing of Heaven.

This, Sir, was a time when you clearly saw into the injustice of a state of slavery, and in which you had just apprehensions of the horrors of its condition. It was now that your abhorrence thereof was so excited, that you publicly held forth this true and invaluable doctrine, which is worthy to be recorded and remembered in all succeeding ages: "We hold these truths to be self-evident, that all men are created equal; that they are endowed by their Creator with certain unalienable rights, and that among these are, life, liberty, and the pursuit of happiness." Here was a time, in which your tender feelings for yourselves had engaged you thus to declare, you were then impressed with proper ideas of the great violation of liberty, and the free possession of those blessings, to which you were entitled by nature; but, Sir, how pitiable is it to reflect, that although you were so fully convinced of the benevolence of the Father of Mankind, and of his equal and impartial distribution of these rights and privileges, which he hath conferred upon them, that you should at the same time counteract his mercies, in detaining by fraud and violence so numerous a part of my brethren, under groaning captivity and cruel oppression, that you should at the same time be found guilty of that most criminal act, which you professedly detested in others, with respect to yourselves.

I suppose that your knowledge of the situation of my brethren, is too extensive to need a recital here; neither shall I presume to prescribe methods by which they may be relieved, otherwise than by recommending to you and all others, to wean yourselves from those narrow prejudices which you have imbibed with respect to them, and as Job proposed to his friends, "put your soul in their souls' stead;" thus shall your hearts be enlarged with kindness and benevolence towards them; and thus shall you need neither the direction of myself or others, in what manner to proceed herein. And now, Sir, although my sympathy and affection for my brethren hath caused my enlargement thus far, I ardently hope, that your candor and generosity will plead with you in my behalf, when I make known to you, that it was not originally my design; but having taken up my pen in order to direct to you, as a present, a copy of an Almanac, which I have calculated for the succeeding year, I was unexpectedly and unavoidably led thereto.

This calculation is the production of my arduous study, in this my advanced stage of life; for having long had unbounded desires to become acquainted with the secrets of nature, I have had to gratify my curiosity herein, through my own assiduous application to Astronomical Study, in which I need not recount to you the many difficulties and disadvantages, which I have had to encounter.

And although I had almost declined to make my calculation for the ensuing year, in consequence of that time which I had allotted therefor, being taken up at the Federal Territory, by the request of Mr. Andrew Ellicott, yet finding myself under several engagements to Printers of this state, to whom I had communicated my design, on my return to my place of residence, I industriously applied myself thereto, which I hope I have accomplished with correctness and accuracy; a copy of which I have taken the liberty to direct to you, and which I humbly request you will favorably receive; and although you may have the opportunity of perusing it after its publication, yet I choose to send it to you in manuscript previous thereto, that thereby you might not only have an earlier inspection, but that you might also view it in my own hand writing.

And now, Sir, I shall conclude, and subscribe myself, with the most profound respect, Your most obedient humble servant[. . .]

To Benjamin Banneker
Philadelphia, August 30, 1791

Sir, – I thank you sincerely for your letter of the 19th instant and for the Almanac it contained. No body wishes more than I do to see such proofs as you exhibit, that nature has given to our black brethren, talents equal to those of the other colors of men, and that the appearance of a want of them is owing merely to the degraded condition of their existence, both in Africa & America. I can add with truth, that no body wishes more ardently to see a good system commenced for raising the condition both of their body & mind to what it ought to be, as fast as the imbecility of their present existence, and other circumstances which cannot be neglected, will admit. I have taken the liberty of sending your Almanac to Monsieur de Condorcet, Secretary of the Academy of Sciences at Paris, and member of the Philanthropic society, because I considered it as a document to which your whole colour had a right for their justification against the doubts which have been entertained of them. I am with great esteem, Sir Your most obed't humble serv't.[. . .]

To the Governor of Virginia, James Monroe
Washington, November 24, 1801

Dear Sir, – I had not been unmindful of your letter of June 15, covering a resolution of the House of Representatives of Virginia, and referred to in yours of the 17th inst. The importance of the subject, and the belief that it gave us time for consideration till the next meeting of the Legislature, have induced me to defer the answer to this date. You will perceive that some circumstances connected with the subject, & necessarily presenting themselves to view, would be improper but for yours' & the legislative ear. Their publication might have an ill effect in more than one quarter. In confidence of attention to this, shall indulge greater freedom in writing.

Common malefactors, I presume, make no part of the object of that resolution. Neither their numbers, nor the nature of their offences, seem to require any provisions beyond those practised heretofore, & found adequate to the repression of ordinary crimes. Conspiracy, insurgency, treason, rebellion, among that description of persons who brought on us the alarm, and on themselves the tragedy, of 1800, were doubtless within the view of every one; but many perhaps contemplated, and one expression of the resolution might comprehend, a much larger scope. Respect to both opinions makes it my duty to understand the resolution in all the extent of which it is susceptible.

The idea seems to be to provide for these people by a purchase of lands; and it is asked whether such a purchase can be made of the US in their western territory? A very great extent of country, north of the Ohio, has been laid off into townships, and is now at market, according to the provisions of the acts of Congress, with which you are acquainted. There is nothing which would restrain the State of Virginia either in the purchase or the application of these lands; but a purchase, by the acre, might perhaps be a more expensive provision than the H of Representatives contemplated. Questions would also arise whether the establishment of such a colony within our limits, and to become a part of our union, would be desirable to the State of Virginia itself, or to the other States – especially those who would be in its vicinity?

Could we procure lands beyond the limits of the US to form a receptacle for these people? On our northern boundary, the country not occupied by British subjects, is the property of Indian nations, whose title would be to be extinguished, with the consent of Great Britain; & the new settlers would be British subjects. It is hardly to be believed that either Great Britain or the Indian proprietors have so disinterested a regard for us, as to be willing to relieve us, by receiving such a colony themselves; and as much to be doubted whether that race of men could long exist in so rigorous a climate. On our western & southern frontiers, Spain holds an immense country, the occupancy of which, however, is in the Indian natives, except a few insulated spots possessed by Spanish subjects. It is very questionable, indeed, whether the Indians would sell? whether Spain would be willing to receive these people? and nearly certain that she would not alienate the sovereignty. The same question to ourselves would recur here also, as did in the first case: should we be willing to have such a colony in contact with us? However our present interests may restrain us within our own limits, it is impossible not to look forward to distant times, when our rapid multiplication will expand itself beyond those limits, & cover the whole northern, if not the southern continent, with a people speaking the same language, governed in similar forms, & by similar laws; nor can we contemplate with satisfaction either blot or mixture on that surface. Spain, France, and Portugal hold possessions on the southern continent, as to which I am not well enough informed to say how far they might meet our views. But either there or in the northern continent, should the constituted authorities of Virginia fix their attention, of preference, I will have the dispositions of those powers sounded in the first instance.

The West Indies offer a more probable & practicable retreat for them. Inhabited already by a people of their own race & color; climates congenial with their natural constitution; insulated from the other descriptions of men; nature seems to have formed these islands to become the receptacle of the blacks transplanted into this hemisphere. Whether we could obtain from the European sovereigns of those islands leave to send thither the persons under consideration, I cannot say; but I think it more probable than the former propositions, because of their being already inhabited more or less by the same race. The most promising portion of them is the island of St. Domingo, where the blacks are established into a sovereignty *de facto*, & have organized themselves under regular laws & government. I should conjecture that their present ruler might be willing, on many considerations, to receive even that description which would be exiled for acts deemed criminal by us, but meritorious, perhaps, by him. The possibility that these exiles might stimulate & conduct vindicative or predatory descents on our coasts, & facilitate concert with their brethren remaining here, looks to a state of things between that island & us not probable on a contemplation of our relative strength, and of the disproportion daily growing; and it is overweighed by the humanity of the measures proposed, & the advantages of disembarrassing ourselves of such dangerous characters. Africa would offer a last & undoubted resort, if all others more desirable should fail us. Whenever the Legislature of Virginia shall have brought it's mind to a point, so that I may know exactly what to propose to foreign authorities, I will execute their wishes with fidelity & zeal. I hope, however, they will pardon me for suggesting a single question for their own consideration. When we contemplate the variety of countries & of sovereigns towards which we may direct our views, the vast revolutions & changes of circumstances which are now in a course of progression, the possibilities that arrangements now to be made, with a view to any particular plan, may, at no great distance of time, be totally deranged by a change of sovereignty, of government, or of other circumstances, it will be for the Legislature to consider whether, after they shall have made all those general provisions which may be fixed by legislative authority, it would be reposing too much confidence in their Executive to leave the place of relegation to be decided on by *them*. They could accommodate their arrangements to the actual state of things, in which countries or powers may be found to exist at the day; and may prevent the effect of the law from being defeated by intervening changes. This, however, is for them to decide. Our duty will be to respect their decision.[. . .]

To Brother Handsome Lake
November 3, 1802

[. . .] You remind me, brother, of what I said to you, when you visited me the last winter, that the lands you then held would remain yours, and shall never go from you but when you should be disposed to sell. This I now repeat, and will ever abide by. We, indeed, are always ready to buy land; but we will never ask but when you wish to sell; and our laws, in order to protect you against imposition, have forbidden individuals to purchase land from you; and have rendered it necessary, when you desire to sell, even to a State, that an agent from the United States should attend the sale, see that your consent is freely given, a satisfactory price paid, and report to us what has been done, for our approbation. This was done in the late case of which you complain. The deputies of your nation came forward, in all the forms which we have been used to consider as evidence of the will of your nation. They proposed to sell to the State of New York certain parcels of land, of small extent, and detached from the body of your other lands; the State of New York was desirous to buy. I sent an agent, in whom we could trust, to see that your consent was free, and the sale fair. All was reported to be free and fair. The lands were your property. The right to sell is one of the rights of property. To forbid you the exercise of that right would be wrong to your nation. Nor do I think, brother, that the sale of lands is, under all circumstances, injurious to your people. While they depended on hunting, the more extensive the forest around them, the more game they would yield. But going into a state of agriculture, it may be as advantageous to a society, as it is to an individual, who has more land than he can improve, to sell a part, and lay out the money in stocks and implements of agriculture, for the better improvement of the residue. A little land well stocked and improved, will yield more than a great deal without stock or improvement. I hope, therefore, that on further reflection, you will see this transaction in a more favorable light, both as it concerns the interest of your nation, and the exercise of that superintending care which I am sincerely anxious to employ for their subsistence and happiness. Go on then, brother, in the great reformation you have undertaken. Persuade our red brethren then to be sober, and to cultivate their lands; and their women to spin and weave for their families. You will soon see your women and children well fed and clothed, your men living happily in peace and plenty, and your numbers increasing from year to year. It will be a great glory to you to have been the instrument of so happy a change, and your children's children, from generation to generation, will repeat your name with love and gratitude forever. In all your enterprises for the good of your people, you may count with confidence on the aid and protection of the United States, and on the sincerity and zeal with which I am myself animated in the furthering of this humane work. You are our brethren of the same land; we wish your prosperity as brethren should do. Farewell.[. . .]

To Benjamin Hawkins
Washington, February 18, 1803

Dear Sir, [. . .] Altho' you will receive, thro' the official channel of the War Office, every communication necessary to develop to you our views respecting the Indians, and to direct your conduct, yet, supposing it will be satisfactory to you, and to those with whom you are placed, to understand my personal dispositions and opinions in this particular, I shall avail myself of this private letter to state them generally. I consider the business of hunting as already become insufficient to furnish clothing and subsistence to the Indians. The promotion of agriculture, therefore, and household manufacture, are essential in their preservation, and I am disposed to aid and encourage it liberally. This will enable them to live on much smaller portions of land, and indeed will render their vast forests useless but for the range of cattle; for which purpose, also, as they become better farmers, they will be found useless, and even disadvantageous. While they are learning to do better on less land, our increasing numbers will be calling for more land, and thus a coincidence of interests will be produced between those who have lands to spare, and want other necessaries, and those who have such necessaries to spare, and want lands. This commerce, then, will be for the good of both, and those who are friends to both ought to encourage it. You are in the station peculiarly charged with this interchange, and who have it peculiarly in your power to promote among the Indians a sense of the superior value of a little land, well cultivated, over a great deal, unimproved, and to encourage them to make this estimate truly. The wisdom of the animal which amputates & abandons to the hunter the parts for which he is pursued should be theirs, with this difference, that the former sacrifices what is useful, the latter what is not. In truth, the ultimate point of rest & happiness for them is to let our settlements and theirs meet and blend together, to intermix, and become one people. Incorporating themselves with us as citizens of the U.S., this is what the natural progress of things will of course bring on, and it will be better to promote than to retard it. Surely it will be better for them to be identified with us, and preserved in the occupation of their lands, than be exposed to the many casualties which may endanger them while a separate people. I have little doubt but that your reflections must have led you to view the various ways in which their history may terminate, and to see that this is the one most for their happiness. And we have already had an application from a settlement of Indians to become citizens of the US. It is possible, perhaps probable, that this idea may be so novel as that it might shock the Indians, were it even hinted to them. Of course, you will keep it for your own reflection; but, convinced of its soundness, feel it consistent with pure morality to lead them towards it, to familiarize them to the idea that it is for their interest to cede lands at times to the US, and for us thus to procure gratifications to our citizens, from time to time, by new acquisitions of land.[. . .]

To Governor William H. Harrison
Washington, February 27, 1803

Dear Sir, [. . .] You will receive herewith an answer to your letter
as President of the Convention; and from the Secretary of War you
receive from time to time information and instructions as to our
Indian affairs. These communications being for the public records,
are restrained always to particular objects and occasions; but this letter
being unofficial and private, I may with safety give you a more
extensive view of our policy respecting the Indians, that you may the
better comprehend the parts dealt out to you in detail through the
official channel, and observing the system of which they make a part,
conduct yourself in unison with it in cases where you are obliged to
act without instruction. Our system is to live in perpetual peace with
the Indians, to cultivate an affectionate attachment from them, by
everything just and liberal which we can do for them within the
bounds of reason, and by giving them effectual protection against
wrongs from our own people. The decrease of game rendering their
subsistence by hunting insufficient, we wish to draw them to agriculture, to spinning and weaving. The latter branches they take up
with great readiness, because they fall to the women, who gain by
quitting the labors of the field for those which are exercised within
doors. When they withdraw themselves to the culture of a small piece
of land, they will perceive how useless to them are their extensive
forests, and will be willing to pare them off from time to time in
exchange for necessaries for their farms and families. To promote this
disposition to ex-change lands, which they have to spare and we want,
for necessaries, which we have to spare and they want, we shall push

our trading uses, and be glad to see the good and influential individuals among them run in debt, because we ob-serve that when these debts get beyond what the individuals can pay, they become willing to lop them off by a cession of lands. At our trading houses, too, we mean to sell so low as merely to repay us cost and charges, so as neither to lessen or enlarge our capital. This is what private traders cannot do, for they must gain; they will consequently retire from the competition, and we shall thus get clear of this pest without giving offence or umbrage to the Indians. In this way our settlements will gradually circumscribe and approach the Indians, and they will in time either incorporate with us as citizens of the United States, or remove beyond the Mississippi. The former is certainly the termination of their history most happy for themselves; but, in the whole course of this, it is essential to cultivate their love. As to their fear, we presume that our strength and their weakness is now so visible that they must see we have only to shut our hand to crush them, and that all our liberalities to them proceed from motives of pure humanity only. Should any tribe be fool-hardy enough to take up the hatchet at any time, the seizing the whole country of that tribe, and driving them across the Mississippi, as the only condition of peace, would be an example to others, and a furtherance of our final consolidation.[. . .]

To Edward Coles
Monticello, August 25, 1814

Dear Sir, – Your favour of July 31, was duly received, and was read with peculiar pleasure. The sentiments breathed through the whole do honor to both the head and heart of the writer. Mine on the subject of slavery of negroes have long since been in possession of the public, and time has only served to give them stronger root. The love of justice and the love of country plead equally the cause of these people, and it is a moral reproach to us that they should have pleaded it so long in vain, and should have produced not a single effort, nay fear not much serious willingness to relieve them & ourselves from our present condition of moral & political reprobation. From those of the former generation who were in the fulness of age when I came into public life, which was while our controversy with England was on paper only, I soon saw that nothing was to be hoped. Nursed and educated in the daily habit of seeing the degraded condition, both bodily and mental, of those unfortunate beings, not reflecting that that degradation was very much the work of themselves & their fathers, few minds have yet doubted but that they were as legitimate subjects of property as their horses and cattle. The quiet and monotonous course of colonial life has been disturbed by no alarm, and little reflection on the value of liberty. And when alarm was taken at an enterprize on their own, it was not easy to carry them to the whole length of the principles which they invoked for themselves. In the first or second session of the Legislature after I became a member, drew to this subject the attention of Col. Bland, one of the oldest, ablest, & most respected members, and he undertook to move for certain moderate extensions of the protection of the laws to these people. I seconded his motion, and, as a younger member, was more spared in the debate; but he was denounced as an enemy of his country, & was treated with the grossest indecorum. From an early stage of our revolution other & more distant duties were assigned to me, so that from that time till my return from Europe in 1789, and I may say till I returned to reside at home in 1809, I had little opportunity of knowing the progress of public sentiment here on this subject. I had always hoped that the younger generation receiving their early impressions after the flame of liberty had been kindled in every breast, & had become as it were the vital spirit of every American, that the generous temperament of youth, analogous to the motion of their blood, and above the suggestions of avarice, would have sympathized with oppression wherever found, and proved their love of liberty beyond their own share of it. But my intercourse with them, since my return has not been sufficient to ascertain that they had made towards this point the progress I had hoped. Your solitary but welcome voice is the first which has brought this sound to my ear; and I have considered the general silence which prevails on this subject as indicating an apathy unfavorable to every hope. Yet the hour of emancipation is advancing, in the march of time. It will come; and whether brought on by the generous energy of our own minds; or by the bloody process of St Domingo, excited and conducted by the power of our present enemy, if once stationed permanently within our Country, and offering asylum & arms to the oppressed, is a leaf of our history not yet turned over. As to the method by which this difficult work is to be effected, if permitted to be done by ourselves, I have seen no proposition so expedient on the whole, as that as emancipation of those born after a given day, and of their education and expatriation after a given age. This would give time for a gradual extinction of that species of labour & substitution of another, and lessen the severity of the shock which an operation so fundamental cannot fail to produce. For men probably of any color, but of this color we know, brought from their infancy without necessity for thought or forecast, are by their habits rendered as incapable as children of taking care of themselves, and are extinguished promptly wherever industry is necessary for raising young. In the mean time they are pests in society by their idleness, and the depredations to which this leads them. Their amalgamation with the other color produces a degradation to which no lover of his country, no lover of excellence in the human character can innocently consent. I am sensible of the partialities with which you have looked towards me as the person who should undertake this salutary but arduous work. But this, my dear sir, is like bidding old Priam to buckle the armour of Hector "trementibus aequo humeris et inutile ferruncingi." No, have overlived the generation with which mutual labors & perils begat mutual confidence and influence. This enterprise is for the young; for those who can follow it up, and bear it through to its consummation. It shall have all my prayers, & these are the only weapons of an old man. But in the mean time are you right in abandoning this property, and your country with it? I think not. My opinion has ever been that, until more can be done for them, we should endeavor, with those whom fortune has thrown on our hands, to feed and clothe them well, protect them from all ill usage, require such reasonable labor only as is performed voluntarily by freemen, & be led by no repugnancies to abdicate them, and our duties to them. The laws do not permit us to turn them loose, if that were for their good: and to commute them for other property is to commit them to those whose usage of them we cannot control. I hope then, my dear sir, you will reconcile yourself to your country and its unfortunate condition; that you will not lessen its stock of sound disposition by withdrawing your portion from the mass. That, on the contrary you will come forward in the public councils, become the missionary of this doctrine truly christian; insinuate & inculcate it softly but steadily, through the medium of writing and conversation; associate others in your labors, and when the phalanx is formed, bring on and press the proposition perseveringly until its accomplishment. It is an encouraging observation that no good measure was ever proposed, which, if duly pursued, failed to prevail in the end. We have proof of this in the history of the endeavors in the English parliament to suppress that very trade which brought this evil on us. And you will be supported by the religious precept, "be not weary in well-doing." That your success may be as speedy & complete, as it will be of honorable & immortal consolation to yourself, I shall as fervently and sincerely pray as I assure you of my great friendship and respect.[. . .]

To John Holmes
Monticello, April 22, 1820

I thank you, dear Sir, for the copy you have been so kind as to send
me of the letter to your constituents on the Missouri question. It is
a perfect justification to them. I had for a long time ceased to read
newspapers, or pay any attention to public affairs, confident they were
in good hands, and content to be a passenger in our bark to the shore
from which I am not distant. But this momentous question, like a
fire bell in the night, awakened and filled me with terror. I considered
it at once as the knell of the Union. It is hushed, indeed, for the
moment. But this is a reprieve only, not a final sentence. A geographical
line, coinciding with a marked principle, moral and political, once
conceived and held up to the angry passions of men, will never be
obliterated; and every new irritation will mark it deeper and deeper.
I can say, with conscious truth, that there is not a man on earth who
would sacrifice more than I would to relieve us from this heavy
reproach, in any *practicable* way. The cession of that kind of property,
for so it is misnamed, is a bagatelle which would not cost me a second
thought, if, in that way, a general emancipation and *expatriation* could
be effected; and gradually, and with due sacrifices, I think it might
be. But as it is, we have the wolf by the ears, and we can neither
hold him, nor safely let him go. Justice is in one scale, and self-
preservation in the other. Of one thing I am certain, that as the passage
of slaves from one State to another, would not make a slave of a
single human being who would not be so without it, so their diffusion
over a greater surface would make them individually happier, and
proportionally facilitate the accomplishment of their emancipation, by

dividing the burthen on a greater number of coadjutors. An abstinence too, from this act of power, would remove the jealousy excited by the undertaking of Congress to regulate the condition of the different descriptions of men composing a State. This certainly is the exclusive right of every State, which nothing in the constitution has taken from them and given to the General Government. Could Congress, for example, say, that the non-freemen of Connecticut shall be freemen, or that they shall not emigrate into any other State?

I regret that I am now to die in the belief, that the useless sacrifice of themselves by the generation of 1776, to acquire self-government and happiness to their country, is to be thrown away by the unwise and unworthy passions of their sons, and that my only consolation is to be, that I live not to weep over it. If they would but dispassionately weigh the blessings they will throw away, against an abstract principle more likely to be effected by union than by scission, they would pause before they would perpetrate this act of suicide on themselves, and of treason against the hopes of the world. To yourself, as the faithful advocate of the Union, I tender the offering of my high esteem and respect.[. . .]

To Jared Sparks
Monticello, February 4, 1824

Dear Sir, – I duly received your favor of the 13th, and with it, the last number of the North American Review. This has anticipated the one I should receive in course, but have not yet received, under my subscription to the new series. The article on the African colonization of the people of color, to which you invite my attention, I have read with great consideration. It is, indeed, a fine one, and will do much good. I learn from it more, too, than I had before known, of the degree of success and promise of that colony.

In the disposition of these unfortunate people, there are two rational objects to be distinctly kept in view. First. The establishment of a colony on the coast of Africa, which may introduce among the aborigines the arts of cultivated life, and the blessings of civilization and science. By doing this, we may make to them some retribution for the long course of injuries we have been committing on their population. And considering that these blessings will descend to the *"nati natorum, et qui nascentur ab illis,"* we shall in the long run have rendered them perhaps more good than evil. To fulfil this object, the colony of Sierra Leone promises well, and that of Mesurado adds to our prospect of success. Under this view, the colonization society is to be considered as a missionary society, having in view, however, objects more humane, more justifiable, and less aggressive on the peace of other nations, than the others of that appellation.

The subject object, and the most interesting to us, as coming home to our physical and moral characters, to our happiness and safety, is to provide an asylum to which we can, by degrees, send the whole of that population from among us, and establish them under our patronage and protection, as a separate, free and independent people, in some country and climate friendly to human life and happiness. That any place on the coast of Africa should answer the latter purpose, I have ever deemed entirely impossible. And without repeating the other arguments which have been urged by others, I will appeal to figures only, which admit no controversy. I shall speak in round numbers, not absolutely accurate, yet not so wide from truth as to vary the result materially. There are in the United States a million and a half of people of color in slavery. To send off the whole of these at once, nobody conceives to be practicable for us, or expedient for them. Let us take twenty-five years for its accomplishment, within which time they will be doubled. Their estimated value as property, in the first place, (for actual property has been lawfully vested in that form, and who can lawfully take it from the possessors?) at an average of two hundred dollars each, young and old, would amount to six hundred millions of dollars, which must be paid or lost by somebody. To this, add the cost of their transportation by land and sea to Mesurado, a year's provision of food and clothing, implements of husbandry and of their trades, which will amount to three hundred millions more, making thirty-six millions of dollars a year for twenty-five years, with insurance of peace all that time, and it is impossible to look at the question a second time. I am aware that at the end of about sixteen years, a gradual detraction from this sum will commence, from the gradual diminution of breeders, and go on during the remaining nine years. Calculate this deduction, and it is still impossible to look at the enterprise a second time. I do not say this to induce an inference that the getting rid of them is forever impossible. For that is neither my opinion nor my hope. But only that it cannot be done in this way. There is, I think, a way in which it can be done; that is, by emancipating the after-born, leaving them, on due compensation, with their mothers, until their services are worth their maintenance, and then putting them to industrious occupations, until a proper age for deportation. This was the result of my reflections on the subject five and forty years ago, and I have never yet been able to conceive any other practicable plan. It was sketched in the Notes on Virginia, under the fourteenth query. The estimated value of the new-born infant is so low, (say twelve dollars and fifty cents,) that it would probably be yielded by the owner gratis, and would thus reduce the six hundred millions of dollars, the first head of expense, to thirty-seven millions and a half; leaving only the expense of nourishment while with the mother, and of transportation. And from what fund are these expenses to be furnished? Why not from that of the lands which have been ceded by the very States now needing this relief? And ceded on no consideration, for the most part, but that of the general good of the whole. These cessions already constitute one fourth of the States of the Union. It may be said that these lands have been sold; are now the property of the citizens composing those States; and the money long ago received and expended. But an equivalent of lands in the territories since acquired, may be appropriated to that object, or so much, at least, as may be sufficient; and the object, although more important to the slave States, is highly so to the others also, if they were serious in their arguments on the Missouri question. The slave States, too, if more interested, would also contribute more by their gratuitous liberation, thus taking on themselves alone the first and heaviest item of expense.

In the plan sketched in the Notes on Virginia, no particular place of asylum was specified; because it was thought possible, that in the revolutionary state of America, then commenced, events might open to us some one within practicable distance. This has now happened. St. Domingo has become independent, and with a population of that color only; and if the public papers are to be credited, their Chief offers to pay their passage, to receive them as free citizens, and to provide them employment. This leaves, then, for the general confederacy, no expense but of nurture with the mother a few years, and would call, of course, for a very moderate appropriation of the vacant lands. Suppose the whole annual increase to be of sixty thousand effective births, fifty vessels, of four hundred tons burthen each, constantly employed in that short run, would carry off the increase of every year, and the old stock would die off in the ordinary course of nature, lessening from the commencement until its final disappearance. In this way no violation of private right is proposed. Voluntary surrenders would probably come in as fast as the means to be provided for their care would be competent to it. Looking at my own State only, and I presume not to speak for the others, I verily believe that this surrender of property would not amount to more, annually, than half our present direct taxes, to be continued fully about twenty or twenty-five years, and then gradually diminishing for as many more until their final extinction; and even this half tax would not be paid in cash, but by the delivery of an object which they have never yet known or counted as part of their property; and those not possessing the object will be called on for nothing. I do not go into all the details of the burthens and benefits of this operation. And who could estimate its blessed effects? I leave this to those who will live to see their accomplishment, and to enjoy a beatitude forbidden to my age. But I leave it with this admonition, to rise and be doing. A million and a half are within their control; but six millions, (which a majority of those now living will see them attain,) and one million of these fighting men, will say, "we will not go."

I am aware that this subject involves some constitutional scruples. But a liberal construction, justified by the object, may go far, and an amendment of the constitution, the whole length necessary. The separation of infants from their mothers, too, would produce some scruples of humanity. But this would be straining at a gnat, and swallowing a camel.

I am much pleased to see that you have taken up the subject of the duty on imported books. I hope a crusade will be kept up against it, until those in power shall become sensible of this stain on our legislation, and shall wipe it from their code, and from the remembrance of man, if possible.

I salute you with assurances of high respect and esteem.[. . .]